PLATING UP PROFIT$

"In *Plating Up Profits*, Bill Hansen shares some gems that apply not only to the world of food and service but to every business endeavor."—Norman Van Aken, chef, author, and recipient of the coveted James Beard "Who's Who of Food & Beverage in America" award

"Bill's book is not just a collection of his experiences but a practical guide for success in the catering and events industry. In fact, entrepreneurs of all types will be inspired by this book."—Klaas De Waal, CEO and publisher of *Catering, Foodservice & Events*

"Bill exceeds his customers' expectations, and this book will exceed yours. It's loaded with stories to motivate and inspire readers to the next level of success!"—J. David Scheiner, retired president of Macy's Florida/Puerto Rico and past chairman of the board of Perry Ellis

"Don't dare call this a book of counseling for caterers (though it is). It is so much more. The lessons within of service and decency and humanity will inspire many. Bill shares a feast full of wisdom."—David Lawrence Jr., retired publisher of the *Miami Herald* and chair of The Children's Movement of Florida

"Bill's book delves into the core principles and practices that effective leaders use to inspire and guide their teams, offering practical advice and real-world examples to help readers develop their leadership skills. I highly recommend it!"—Dr. Michael Cheng, dean at the Chaplin School of Hospitality & Tourism Management at Florida International University

"I can attest to Bill Hansen's mastery of hospitality in creating unforgettable culinary and life experiences. His leadership and teamwork ultimately create the magic that guests experience at his events."—Chef Allen Susser, James Beard Award winner

"Bill Hansen has a wealth of professional and life experiences, which he artfully shares in this most readable book. Reading it will help you be more successful in business and in your personal life."—Sherrill Hudson, retired chairman and CEO of TECO Energy, Inc.

"*Plating Up Profits* is a must-read for aspiring entrepreneurs and seasoned business owners alike, offering invaluable insights on business challenges and achieving long-term success."—Tony Argiz, South Florida managing partner, BDO

"Bill is an icon in our industry. In this book, he shares the good and the bad, the beautiful and the ugly, so all readers can benefit from his experiences."—Peter Schnebly, CEO of Schnebly Winery

"This is a must-read for anyone who wants to sharpen their business acumen and to gain marketplace advantage."—Dr. Mike Hampton, professor and graduate faculty member, Chaplin School of Hospitality & Tourism Management at Florida International University

"Bill has provided many amazing catering events for me at the highest level of quality. More importantly, he helps so many through his philanthropic efforts, and that is what I admire most."—James F. Allen, chairman of Hard Rock International and CEO of Seminole Gaming

"Bill's professional accomplishments speak for themselves … there is much to learn from his experiences. Aside from being a great caterer and businessman, Bill is also a caring and generous member of our community. It is this combination that truly makes him a successful leader."—Alex Penelas, former mayor of Miami-Dade County

"Bill Hansen is one of the true stalwarts of the hospitality industry, having achieved a level of success in the highly competitive catering industry that others could only aspire to. He is a great teacher and mentor."—Carl Sacks, managing partner and senior consultant at Certified Catering Consultants

MIAMI'S CATERING ICON DISHES UP
LESSONS FOR BUSINESS SUCCESS

PLATING UP PROFIT$

BILL HANSEN
WITH
SARA PEREZ WEBBER

First published in 2025 by Bill Hansen with Sara Perez Webber, in partnership with Whitefox Publishing

www.wearewhitefox.com

Copyright © Bill Hansen and Sara Perez Webber, 2025

ISBN 9781917523233
eBook ISBN 9781916797383
Audiobook ISBN 9781916797390

Bill Hansen and Sara Perez Webber assert the moral right to be identified as the authors of this work.

All rights reserved. No part of this publication may be reproduced, stored in a retrieval system or transmitted in any form or by any means, electronic, mechanical, photocopying, recording or otherwise, without prior written permission of the author.

While every effort has been made to trace the owners of copyright material reproduced herein, the author would like to apologize for any omissions and will be pleased to incorporate missing acknowledgments in any future editions.

Designed and typeset by Karen Lilje
Cover design by Emma Ewbank
Project management by Whitefox

To my dearest Terry,

Your unwavering support, dedication, and love have been the bedrock of our lives and the success of our catering business for decades. You've supported the business and me with grace and efficiency, keeping everything in focus while I ventured into writing, teaching, consulting, and even indulging in the occasional golf game at La Gorce Country Club in the '90s. Your strength and perseverance have inspired me every day. This book is as much yours as it is mine. Thank you for being my rock, my partner, and my greatest blessing.

With all my love and gratitude,
Bill

CONTENTS

INTRODUCTION	1
1. PERSEVERANCE: EVERY SETBACK IS A SETUP FOR A COMEBACK	5
How the Personal Impacts the Professional	5
Practice Perseverance in Your Personal and Your Professional Life	8
Consider Each "No" a Step Closer to a "Yes"	10
Seek Continual Improvement	11
Stay Refired, Not Retired	12
Rebound from Financial Setbacks	13
Bounce Back from Bad Investments	15
Survive a Big Event	16
2. SERVICE: THE SECRET INGREDIENT	21
Expect the Unexpected	21
Make Your Clients Feel Valued	24
Be There When Your Clients Are Ready	26
Don't Let High Tech Get in the Way of High Touch	28
Make the Right First Impression	30
Give Them What They Need … and Some Extra for Good Measure	31
Anticipate Customers' Needs	33
Give Your Clients Peace of Mind	36
Pay Attention to Detail	37
Indulge All the Senses	39
After Dropping the Ball, Make a Swift Recovery	41

3. RISK-TAKING: A TURTLE GOES NOWHERE UNTIL IT STICKS ITS NECK OUT   43

    Get Out of Your Comfort Zone and
        Into Your Challenge Zone   43
    When You Stick Your Head Out,
        Take a Good Look Around   46
    Know Your Weaknesses, Strengths, and Tolerance for Risk   48
    In Order to Innovate, Calculate the Risks   51
    Gain a Competitive Advantage by Taking a Risk   53
    Go Deep for a Bigger Catch   57
    You'll Never Know Unless You Try   59

4. SALES AND MARKETING: IF YOU DON'T BOOK IT, YOU CAN'T COOK IT   61

    Find What You're Best At   61
    Set High Standards and Hold Everyone Accountable   62
    Define Your Brand—Then Spread the Word!   65
    Nurture Relationships   70
    Never Stop Sales Training   73
    Get the Most Bang for Your Daily Buck of Time   75
    Teamwork Makes the Sales Dream Work   78
    Vertically Integrate   80

5. TEAMWORK: CULTURE EATS STRATEGY FOR BREAKFAST   83

    Give Employees What They Need   84
    Show Meaningful Appreciation   86
    Focus on Culture Before Hiring   88
    Determine What Your Culture Is   90
    Add Fun to the Mix   93
    Encourage Team Members to Speak Straight   95
    Honor Your Commitments—Even When It's Difficult   96
    Make Quality Personal   98

6. CUSTOMER RELATIONS: HOW TO TAME THE BRIDEZILLA (AND OTHER UNREASONABLE CUSTOMERS) — 101

Treating Staff Members Poorly — 101
Trying to Get a Freebie — 103
Having Champagne Taste on a Beer Budget — 104
Being a Schoolyard Bully — 108
Making Unreasonable Demands — 110
Meddling and Micromanaging — 113

7. QUALITY FIRST: THE BEST ADVERTISING IS ON THE END OF THE FORK — 117

Go the Extra Mile — 117
Define Your Customers Before Defining Your Quality Standards — 120
Be Consistent — 121
Inspect for Greatness Instead of Expecting Greatness — 122
Remember: Quality Starts at the Back Door — 125
Get Involved in the Nitty-Gritty — 127

8. DEALING WITH ADVERSITY: TURN YOUR LEMONS INTO LEMONADE AND LEMON CAKE — 131

Finding Sweetness When the World Turned Sour — 131
Bailing Out Bad Situations — 134
A Spoonful of Sugar Helps the Bitterness Go Down — 137
Keep Calm and Cater On — 139
Solutions, Solutions, Only Solutions — 140
Get to the Root of the Problem — 142

9. STAYING PROFITABLE: IT DON'T MEAN A THING IF IT DON'T GO "KA-CHING!" — 145

Find Those 10 Places Where Money Is Hidden in Your Business — 146
Follow the Lead of Successful Competitors — 148
Keep Your Accounts Receivable Current — 149
Don't Underestimate the Importance of Strong Vendor Relationships — 150
Seek Feedback to Avoid Potential Problems That Could Drag Down Profits — 152
Make Your Cash Work for You — 154
Negotiate Well Now, Save Money Later — 155
Sometimes You Have to Spend to Save — 158

10. LEADERSHIP: GO BIG OR GO HOME — 159

Leaders Make Timely Decisions — 159
Leaders Provide Structure — 162
Leaders Delegate — 163
Leaders Manage Priorities — 165
Leaders Communicate Clearly and Actively Listen — 166
Leaders Show Empathy — 168
Leaders Dream Big … and Then Go for It — 169

ACKNOWLEDGMENTS — 171

INTRODUCTION

If you're a business owner, you and I do the same thing: We cater. We cater to our customers or clients. We cater to our employees (at least, we should). And some of us cater to shareholders. Catering well to your internal and external customers leads to a more harmonious workplace—and higher profits.

In my case, catering is the name of my profession.

During my decades of culinary adventures and misadventures, I've served four U.S. presidents, Pope John Paul II, numerous pop stars, scores of Fortune 500 corporations, and the Masters golf tournament, and I've been a part of more than 10,000 weddings.

I've also had the privilege of getting to know other caterers at the top of their field in cities across the U.S. They've inspired me with their creativity and business know-how for years. Many of them were generous enough to share their insightful stories with me for this book.

You don't have to be a foodie—or a part of the food industry—to find the lessons in this book interesting and relevant. You'll learn about the dynamics of service and problem-solving, which apply to all types of businesses.

When it comes to human behavior, caterers see it all—the good, the bad, the ugly, and the ugliest. After all, we're with our customers during some of their most momentous—and therefore most stressful—times: getting married, watching their children get married, celebrating milestones with their closest family and friends, and saying goodbye to loved ones.

The real-life stories other caterers and I share in this book are meant to be both entertaining and eye-opening. Imagine dealing with a bride whose wedding dress has just been stolen, hours before her ceremony. That type of thing isn't on the menu of typical caterer offerings or responsibilities, but business is a part of life and, as you know, life is messy sometimes.

What might you glean from stories such as the wedding dress incident and others I've included in these pages?

You'll discover how to:

- Satisfy the most difficult of clients.
- Create a service culture that results in engaged employees and delighted customers.
- Take the risks necessary to grow your business.
- Show your customers you care.
- Better anticipate customer needs.
- Recover when customers are unhappy.
- Get rid of a bad employee.
- Keep a good employee.
- Prevent growth that's too fast.
- Kick yourself into drive when you run out of steam.
- Listen to your employees.
- Create a "home" culture at work.
- Deal with unreasonable customers.
- Motivate your team.
- Build your top and bottom lines.

For many business owners, these lessons are more crucial today than ever. The pandemic wreaked havoc with the economy. It turned many industries upside down—particularly the catering and foodservice industries. The caterers who survived were those who were able to quickly change their businesses to reflect the new reality—offering takeout and delivery, for example.

My company not only survived, we're on track to have our biggest years ever in 2024 and 2025. How we did it will be inspirational and instructional for you, no matter what industry you're in.

As far as I know, there's not another book out there written from the perspective of a successful 50-year caterer. I've seen it all, and I share it all. While almost everyone has been on the customer side of a catered event, not many have been on the serving side. In this book, I pull back the curtain to show what goes on behind the scenes.

I began my career in the 1960s at Cornell University, where I graduated from the renowned hotel school. Now, as CEO of Hansen Group and Bill Hansen Catering in Miami, I'm recognized as one of the top 30 caterers in the country. I received one of the most prestigious honors in my profession—the Lifetime Achievement Award from Catersource—and for three decades I've been a part-time college professor in catering management at Florida International University.

In fact, I literally wrote the book on catering; my catering textbook, published by John Wiley & Sons, is now in its third edition.

I've stumbled through my share of roadblocks on the road to success, however. Several years ago, I kicked an addiction to alcohol and prescription drugs after they nearly killed me. Since then, I've recovered my health and taken my business to new heights, proving one of my favorite mantras: You're never too old, and it's never too late to change your life.

To help me tell my story, I've had the good fortune of being able to collaborate with Sara Perez Webber. Since 2010, Sara has been the editor-in-chief and main writer of a magazine for caterers—*Catering, Foodservice & Events* (formerly *Catering Magazine*). She's spoken with many caterers across the country about their business successes and failures. Sara has helped me craft this book's lessons in a way that will appeal to businesspeople of all stripes.

We hope these stories inspire and entertain you. And we hope these lessons help you better cater to your customers, both internal and external, leading to business success and personal satisfaction.

CHAPTER 1
PERSEVERANCE
EVERY SETBACK IS A SETUP FOR A COMEBACK

"When the going gets tough, the tough get going." We've all heard that saying, attributed to Joe Kennedy, father of President John F. Kennedy. But have you ever really thought about its meaning?

When you're at your lowest, when all you want to do is crawl into bed and wish the world away, that's when you need to kick yourself into action. Believe me, I know it's not easy. I've struggled with addictions, financial setbacks, and broken marriages. Yet I'm still in the game in my golden years, playing in the fourth quarter and hopefully into overtime, trying to make each day better than the last, while blessing others with the blessings that I have received.

If it were easy, everyone would do it. The "tough" use each setback as motivation to stage their inevitable comeback.

HOW THE PERSONAL IMPACTS THE PROFESSIONAL

On June 29, 2018—after 45 mg of Adderall during the day and at least seven glasses of bubbly that night—I passed out in my home kitchen, hitting my head on the marble floor. Blood gushed from my scalp, exacerbated by the blood thinner I was taking.

I could have bled out right there on the floor, but my wife Terry (who I call Sugar Girl) found me. She gave me a few chest pumps and mouth-to-mouth and stopped the bleeding. When I woke up, they were loading me into the back of an emergency vehicle on my way to Broward General.

Upon arrival, the nurse got out a huge staple gun and tried to staple the gash on my scalp back together. I joked that he must have flunked his stapling class at Office Depot, since he managed to make me squirm like a schoolboy as he stretched my scalp to put in the staples—without anesthesia.

At a time like that, one can't help thinking, *How did I get to this point?*

Anyone observing from afar on that fateful day in 2018 would have seen a guy in his 70s who'd lived a pretty great life: Ivy League grad, Naval officer, catering business owner through five decades, good husband and father, college professor, book author, spiritual leader, marathon runner, decent golfer with a hole-in-one.

But until that day, there was one big, unspoken albatross around my neck: addiction.

I used alcohol to unwind as soon as the party was over. My team knew that the last thing to pack in the catering truck was the beer cooler stocked with Heineken ("greenies," as my late partner and I called them), since a few of us would chug down a couple before we left the party—just enough for a slight buzz, working up an appetite for a later boozy dinner during the wee hours.

I quit drinking for a couple of years in the mid-1990s as I finished my first book, *Off-Premise Catering Management*, but my deep need for alcoholic libations re-emerged. Before long, I was polishing off a bottle of Chandon Brut sparkling wine each evening before dinner.

Since I had atrial fibrillation, this was against doctor's orders. So I decided to bid farewell to the bottle after a trip to Vegas around 2015. I still remember my last beer before quitting: a 24-ouncer consumed at the Aria Hotel. Cheers.

While in Vegas, I began to feel pain in my mouth. Herpes? Couldn't be. After returning to Miami, the pain got worse. My dentist was no help, so I called my doctor, who told me I had shingles in my mouth. By that time the redness and pain had spread to my face, growing by the day toward my right eye.

If you've had shingles, you know they hurt. (And if you haven't yet, get the shot!) The bad news was the pain. The good news? The OxyContin I began devouring in copious amounts. These capsules compensated for the lack of alcohol in my system, and soon I became addicted, getting them from friends and even with prescriptions before the crackdown on opioid use.

Once an addict, always an addict.

Once my wife discovered opioid charges on my Medicare account, she called my doctor and told him she would turn him in if he prescribed any more to me. So, I quit cold turkey … and drifted back into drinking every night. First one drink, then two, then three … you see where this is going.

All this time, I was operating as a highly functioning alcoholic. Only a handful of folks knew that I needed to get a drink or two as soon as I left work, sometimes even sitting in my car with a beer before I drove home. But I was never arrested for DUI, and the few times I was pulled over for speeding, the cops never made me walk a straight line. (Thank you, breath mints.)

One day, a golfing buddy introduced me to Adderall, which I absolutely loved. I'd be bright-eyed and bushy-tailed all day before coming down with a bottle of bubbly—perhaps preceded by a beer or two.

Business was booming, my family fine, and it seemed I didn't have a care in the world. My dear friend and trainer, Chad Van Allen, used to chide me about these two destructive habits, even as I steadily worked out hard five or six days a week.

But things were not as perfect as they seemed. Sometimes I'd leave work early so I could have a drink or two to relax. Or to connect with my Adderall supplier. I knew I drank too much sometimes at business social events.

Slowly at first—but more urgently week by week as I read my meditations and said morning prayers to my maker—I realized something had to give. If I wanted to make the last quarter century of my life the best it could be, I didn't need to be trying to score Adderall on the street corner and shopping around for the best pricing on Chandon Brut.

In May 2018, I looked up to heaven, begging for any divine help that might be available, since I was not quitting on my own. It came, in a way, a month later when I almost died on my kitchen floor.

Recovery took about six months, and it wasn't easy. But I persevered without alcohol or any unprescribed drugs. In fact, I haven't touched a drop of alcohol since that fateful night.

I could have given in to my addictions—as I had in the past, many times. But finally, at the age of 73, I found the strength to kick the habits that had been haunting me for much of my life.

The next year, I led my company to record-breaking profits.

Coincidence? Not a chance. The strength I tapped into to conquer my personal demons extended into my professional life, helping me to lead my team to greater heights. I wasn't worried anymore about scoring the substances I thought I needed to survive. I could focus fully on the business.

If you're facing a similar battle, take it from me—you can fall many, many times. It's how you pick yourself back up that determines how your story ends.

PRACTICE PERSEVERANCE IN YOUR PERSONAL AND YOUR PROFESSIONAL LIFE

Steve Jobs once said, "I'm convinced that about half of what separates the successful entrepreneurs from the non-successful ones is pure perseverance."

Of course, Jobs is a perfect example. A college dropout, he founded Apple only to lose control of the company after developing the Macintosh. More than a decade later, he triumphantly returned, and changed the world forever when Apple launched the iPhone in 2007.

Where do you stand in the perseverance department? Do you give up easily? When the going gets tough, do you quit? We all do sometimes. But you wouldn't be reading this book—and I wouldn't have written it—if this was our modus operandi.

In my personal life, I've overcome many hurdles. I was a dud in high school athletics, an overweight teen who never shined on the playing field. Yet I ran the New York City Marathon in 1982, coming in just behind the winner that year—Alberto Salazar. Two hours behind him, but you get the picture.

I struck out many times romantically, tying the knot three times before getting it right with my fourth marriage. Terry and I celebrated our 41st wedding anniversary in 2024—and boy am I glad I didn't give up on love before finding her.

As Maya Angelou said, "Do the best you can until you know better. Then when you know better, do better." It's that last bit that many never achieve.

Consider, for example, the common personal goal of weight loss. Many have conceded defeat in the battle of the bulge. And even if they've won the battle, they often lose the war; only one in five people who successfully lose weight can maintain the loss long term.

Researchers from California Polytechnic State University studied over 6,000 members of Weight Watchers who lost more than 50 pounds and kept it off for at least three years. The study found that successful dieters persevered despite setbacks. "Weight-loss maintainers saw setbacks as part of their successful journey," noted Suzanne Phelan, a Cal Poly professor who led the study. "Setbacks were not described as failures. They were seen as a temporary interruption in their path."

In other words, when weight-loss maintainers fell off the wagon, they didn't wallow in the dirt. They got up and back on track—maybe with the next meal or the next day or the next week. These blips didn't end their journey. They were stops that they made on the way to their destination.

Once, my wife asked me why I saved the proposals I didn't win in a file labeled "Learning Experiences." "Sugar Girl," I replied, "I want to learn why I lost the bid so I won't make the same mistake again!"

CONSIDER EACH "NO" A STEP CLOSER TO A "YES"

When Jeffrey Miller was a freshman at the University of Pennsylvania in the 1970s, the young Jewish student found himself with a job he'd never envisioned: selling New Testaments door-to-door.

Day after day, Jeffrey would trudge home without making one sale. He kept at it, however, and soon he was selling one a week—and then more than one a day.

As Jeffrey's sales grew, so did his confidence. So when the time came to pitch what he was truly passionate about—his signature chocolate walnut torte—he was ready.

Jeffrey took one of his cakes to the office of the university's president and asked to see him. The president's gatekeeper declined, saying he was in a lunch meeting, but offered to bring the torte to him. Jeffrey, however, begged for the opportunity to do it himself. Impressed by his moxie, the secretary ushered Jeffrey into the meeting just as the president and his guests were finishing lunch. Perfect timing—they had no dessert.

As the group devoured the delicious torte, Jeffrey handed them his card. The next day, the president's wife called for catering, and the rest is history. Jeffrey A. Miller Catering was born, and for 12 years, it was the preferred caterer for all the various schools and departments at the Ivy League campus. And the company continues to be one of Philadelphia's premier catering and venue firms.

Instead of being intimidated by selling a product that didn't seem to be a natural fit, Jeffrey persisted. His eventual success gave him the confidence to start his own business. Jeffrey's maxim then and now—good advice for anyone in sales—is this: "Every 'no' brings you one step closer to a 'yes.'"

SEEK CONTINUAL IMPROVEMENT

In my business, we're only as good as our last event. While perfection is impossible, excellence is not. That's why we compose a report after every event, detailing what went right—and, more importantly, what went wrong.

By honestly assessing where we failed to measure up, we can focus our efforts on improving those areas for the next event. Most of these things the client doesn't notice, but my team and I do. For example, I want flatware set consistently at the same angles and the same distance from the table's edge. And it drives me crazy when I see photos of chairs pushing the table linens inward rather than just kissing the edge of the cloth.

We're always trying to improve our serving times as well. As most weddings are seated dinners, when we serve is almost as important as what we serve. Have you ever sat at your table, after salads have been cleared, wondering if the main course will ever arrive? Or, worse yet, watching surrounding tables get their meals as you and your tablemates twiddle your thumbs?

I have, and it can ruin a guest's enjoyment. Serving hundreds of people promptly and nearly simultaneously is no easy task—especially since we dish up *à la minute*, avoiding pre-plating and hot boxes. We've got it down to a science, but there's always room for improvement.

One memorable example of fine-tuning an event was in 1995, when we were hired to serve over 10,000 French plumbers and their wives. Seems these foreign flushers were tops in their trade. A plumbing supply company rewarded them with an incentive trip to Miami, where they embarked on a six-day Caribbean cruise. On their last day in town, while awaiting their flights home, they visited the Miami Seaquarium, followed by lunch. That's where we came in.

My company was hired to feed the group as they came through Miami in waves. I still remember that first day when this hungry horde appeared on the horizon, with the Flipper show in the background. It was a sea of humanity.

But my team was ready. We had prepared 10 double-sided buffet lines, and in less than 20 minutes, all 1,300 were seated, enjoying our South Florida barbecue.

Then we repeated the process every six days for eight weeks, improving each time. We tweaked our menu since we had overbought food, streamlined our staffing numbers, and even sped up the lines by pre-setting one dessert at each of the 1,300 place settings, rather than leaving them on the buffet.

By evaluating each lunch—and making the necessary changes—we reduced our labor cost by 10 percent and boosted our gross margin by 13 percent. And the French flushers started their journey back home with tummies full and smiles on their faces.

STAY REFIRED, NOT RETIRED

As I near the age of 80, there is no way I will rest on my laurels. When you do, you begin to die. My idols are those entertainers and even sports stars who keep doing what they love as they age—like the Rolling Stones and Bob Dylan, still touring in their 80s. Or Anthony Hopkins, who won an Oscar at age 83. These legends inspire me to keep on keeping on.

Self-actualization tops the pyramid of Maslow's human needs. And in our later years, if we have nothing to contribute to our self-actualization, part of us begins to deteriorate.

My dad ran a greenhouse business in Western New York. One of his employees, Rudy, loved to fish. He was fishing when the Lord hooked him, and off he traveled on his final fishing trip in the sky. Rudy did what he loved until his last breath—that's something to aspire to.

Bodies in motion stay in motion, and bodies at rest stay at rest. Who wants to be resting all the time?

My friend and mentor Dave Lawrence Jr., a nationally known newspaper editor and publisher of the *Miami Herald* and *Detroit Free Press*, retired at the age of 56. But then he became refired with his second act—as a leading national advocate for children, especially early childhood investment.

Now in his 80s, Dave continues to inspire me when we meet for lunch and share Miami memories. I followed his lead when choosing the charity I devote time and resources to—Touching Miami with Love, which educates and empowers disadvantaged youth in Miami's Overtown neighborhood and Homestead.

At 90 years young, William Shatner starred in romantic comedy *Senior Moments*—an action-packed film featuring fast cars and women half his age. No rocking chairs in sight. And Betty White rocked the world while nearly making it to the age of 100. She hosted *Saturday Night Live* when she was 88!

Inspiration is all around us. Retirement is not an option for me, nor should it be for you. Volunteering, mentoring, working at something you love will extend your life and leave the world a better place.

REBOUND FROM FINANCIAL SETBACKS

Let's face it—when you're an entrepreneur, financial setbacks are a given. Every new business is a roll of the dice. What happens when you crap out, so to speak? Do you give up gambling altogether? If everyone did that, all businesses would eventually fold. Society would collapse.

Half a century ago, I could have easily filed for bankruptcy. I had no job and a mother to support. In early 1971, I was released from active duty as a lieutenant in the U.S. Navy and was offered a stable position—now as a civilian with a major pay raise—managing the Navy Officer's Club facilities in the Hotel Del Monte in Monterey, California.

I excelled at this job and loved every minute of it. After a while, however, I was approached by some colleagues to start a hotel-restaurant systems consulting firm. My entrepreneurial drive took over, I invested $5,000 for a small percentage of the firm, and Spectra Cybernetics was born. Soon our clients included the Sahara Hotel in Las Vegas, Harveys Lake Tahoe, the Pebble Beach Golf Club, and the run-down Mapes Hotel in Reno.

Money was pouring in—but pouring out faster. One of our employees stole a partner's Lincoln Continental along with my Mobil Oil credit card and fled to the East Coast. He was finally apprehended when he tried to charge tires to the card and sent to prison. But prison time did not pay my bills.

I'd gone months without a paycheck, and all five of my credit cards were charged to the max. Burdened with student debt, I also had to pay back the $5,000 I invested in the firm—a loan from my friend's dad. On my last day in Reno—which happened to be Thanksgiving Day—I ate a lonely breakfast at the Mapes Hotel, watching another patron win the big keno prize of $25,000. It could have been me.

With my tail between my legs, my only option was to go back to the Carmel Valley and live with my mom. On the way there, I was literally "Stuck in Lodi," like the Creedence Clearwater Revival song. When my Mercury Marquis Brougham broke down, I celebrated Thanksgiving with a turkey sandwich from the Greyhound bus station vending machine.

Broke, busted, and disgusted. But not for long.

Here's how I rebounded in less than a month.

I started dialing for dollars, and within three weeks, I'd landed a job working for the Navy's Bureau of Personnel as a traveling consultant. Slowly I made good on my debts through sheer perseverance rather than taking the easy way out and filing for bankruptcy.

Everyone suffers financial setbacks. To bounce back, you must:

- Accept your situation. It is what it is, as they say.
- Prepare a budget, with expenses whittled down to the basics.
- Reach out to your creditors, if you owe money. *Be proactive, not reactive!* Let them know you're in a bind, that you will pay

them, but you need their cooperation. Waiting for them to attack you for the money will put you on the defensive.
- Look on your setback as a learning experience, once the dust has settled. Don't make the same mistakes twice!

Yes, it's painful. But think of it as running a road race. You struggle through shortness of breath, aching muscles and joints, dehydration, and inclines that seem to go on forever, but it's all worth it when you cross that finish line to the cheers of your friends and family, with a medal waiting for you ... and perhaps even a cold adult beverage!

Focus on the prize.

BOUNCE BACK FROM BAD INVESTMENTS

In 2006, a long stretch of beach in a state park on the Atlantic just south of Fort Lauderdale had me seeing dollar signs. I invested in a concession business there, which included a snack bar along the southern part of the park. The potential was amazing for weekend business, and I had visions of nonstop beachfront corporate and social events in the sand. Sweetening the deal, the seller of the concession had business already booked, which helped offset the mid-six-figure purchase price.

Unfortunately, I was building sandcastles in the sky.

Learn from my mistake—do your due diligence! I didn't, so was unaware that outdoor lights could only be used at nighttime events for four months each year (to protect nesting sea turtles). Nor did I understand that alcoholic beverages couldn't be served on the beach from sunup to sundown.

One apparent bright light was a catamaran with tourists that docked in the park as many as five days a week. We prepared up to 50 box lunches per day for guests while they explored the park. But then a storm battered the dock, and the catamaran visits stopped. And Mother Nature continued her assault—a waterspout destroyed my 80-foot tent. I finally gave up, walking away from a five-year contract with two years remaining.

Not all deals that appear sunny stay that way, as dark clouds can move in to take away your profits.

So how can you move forward after a bad investment?

- First, stop the negative thinking. Negative thoughts equal negative results. Focus on what did work out and move forward.
- Get help! Find a mastermind group like Entrepreneurs' Organization or Vistage to coach you to success in your next business venture.
- Get some space. Don't jump right into the next investment. Step back and regroup.
- Reflect. Think about the *why* behind your investments and other business moves. I journal every day, which helps me keep things in perspective—both in good times and bad.
- Look at your business failure as a learning experience. What lessons can you take away that will help you succeed in the future? Forget the mistake and remember the lesson.

SURVIVE A BIG EVENT

Sometimes, major setbacks are completely out of your control. Recessions, natural disasters, pandemics … they're inevitable and no one is exempt.

I've lived through the war in Vietnam, the gas shortage in the mid '70s, the recession in the late '80s, 9/11, the Great Recession, hurricanes, a serious Zika virus, and—of course—the COVID pandemic.

My survival skills are deeply embedded in my being. And my attitude is that every setback is a setup for a comeback.

When 9/11 stymied my catering business, I focused on my new brand: Leading Caterers of America (LCA), a consortium of top caterers in the U.S. and Canada. Under the LCA brand, I led catering boot camps from coast to coast, coaching caterers on ways to build their sales and reduce their costs. That helped to make up for the loss of revenue from catering.

When the Great Recession hit in 2008/2009, our sales plummeted by 30 percent. We were headed into negative number territory when we were "saved" by being hired to provide lunches for two Catholic schools. Praise the Lord!

The dreaded Zika virus hit South Florida in the mid-teens. As the British newspaper *The Guardian* reported: "With the number of confirmed Zika cases continuing to rise, and the peak winter tourism season barely two months away, fears are growing that publicity over the mosquito-borne disease could put visitors off and deliver a hard hit to [Miami's] $24bn tourism industry."

Hit hard it did. Weddings and corporate meetings shied away from Miami, and our sales plunged 40 percent. Unfortunately, I had to lay off many team members to stay afloat … and it hurt me as much as it did them.

We got back on our feet and soared into 2020, on our way to our best year ever. Then, in March, COVID hit, wiping out our wedding and event schedule for months.

Surviving economic setbacks is part of the game of business. It's not always champagne and caviar. Sometimes it's Tang and Spam.

When business suffers a setback due to circumstances beyond our control, I've learned to focus on the following principles:

1. Scrutinize each fixed cost.
Lowering your expenses is key to survival. Can you negotiate a lower rent? Are there team members on your payroll that are non-essential? Can you reduce salaries for the short term? Ask your insurance agent if your premiums have decreased due to lower sales. Examine every aspect of your business, and trim where you can.

2. Don't cut back on sales and marketing.
When COVID erased our catered event schedule, we pivoted into meal deliveries, like many others in the business. Unlike many competitors, however, we did not cut back on our sales and marketing

efforts. Instead, we used PPP and SBA loan money to boost spending in these areas.

When the pandemic slowed, this move paid off in spades. Couples who had put off their weddings were anxious to tie the knot. Many chose to wed in South Florida, as we didn't have the tight restrictions many other states enacted during the pandemic. And when they searched online for caterers and venues, they found us, because we had invested in our marketing strategies. Bill Hansen Catering was ready and waiting for their business. For many weeks, our venue, Villa Woodbine, was booked with weddings every day of the week.

3. Never forget: Cash is king.
Cash is king. Cash is king. Repeat this as your mantra during tough times. You must have liquidity to survive.

4. Take advantage of growth opportunities.
During tough economic times, if you have cash and good credit, opportunities for expanding your business through mergers and acquisitions abound. For nearly four decades, my wife Terry and I owned and operated our one business: Bill Hansen Catering. Around 2018, however, we dipped our toes into expansion. And when COVID reared its ugly head, causing many caterers to sadly shut their doors, we were able to acquire what others were desperate to offload. Here are some moves we made:

- First, we purchased Catering by Lovables, a brand that now operates out of our commissary but offers catering at a lower price point than Bill Hansen Catering.
- A year later—after the pandemic hit—the owners of Eten Catering decided to move back to England. The owners had relationships with clients in the yachting and corporate worlds that I did not have, so there was no value to the business without a transition period. Remember, people buy from people they know. From England, Allison Morgan and her husband, Dirk, continued to sell remotely while my team in Miami delivered

the catering. This deal was structured with little cash down, but a higher commission paid out over three years.
- During COVID and after—with the shortage of culinary, service, and operations workers—staffing agencies like Instawork, Qwick, and others flourished as caterers and other firms paid a premium while these firms generated amazing profits. Well, if you can't beat 'em, join 'em, I always say. I partnered with a start-up staffing agency, Staff305, in mid-2022, but soon decided that we were better off focusing on recruiting and training our own staff members.

Clearly, there is risk in all these investments, but they are calculated risks. And I'm a risk-taker. If you don't grow, you begin to die.

Keep in mind that integrating acquisitions into your existing business takes time. Communication is critical. New employees need to understand your mission, vision, and core values—and be on board as team players. Customers must be informed of all changes. You may lose employees and customers that came with the acquisitions. That's OK; they'll find a better fit.

What you stand to gain will more than make up for any losses—increased revenue while saving costs through combined sales, marketing, accounting, financing, purchasing, and production operations.

CHAPTER 2
SERVICE
THE SECRET INGREDIENT

I'LL LET YOU IN ON a catering secret: Service is more important to guest satisfaction than food. That was the consensus in a survey I conducted of 625 meeting and event planners, and it's something I've always known instinctively.

Service is all about how you make your customers and guests feel. Fellow Cornell grad Will Guidara authored a bestselling book titled *Unreasonable Hospitality*, detailing the remarkable power of giving people more than they expect as he piloted New York's Eleven Madison Park to number one on the World's Best Restaurant list. His book inspires me and underscores my belief about good service: When we make people feel good about themselves and about us, success follows exponentially.

EXPECT THE UNEXPECTED

I cut my off-premise catering teeth working at Vizcaya Museum and Gardens, a waterfront mansion on Miami's Biscayne Bay overlooking Key Biscayne and a handful of homes called Stiltsville—which are literally built on stilts in the shallow offshore waters.

Catering at Vizcaya is not for the faint-hearted. Built in the early 1900s as the winter home of James Deering, cofounder of International Harvester, the lavish mansion's kitchens are off-limits. You get three hours to build a kitchen some 100 yards from the water's edge dining area—and set up all the tables, chairs, place settings, bars, and buffets on the terrace.

If dining inside, you only have one hour to set up before guests arrive.

So the stress level was high as we prepped for a wedding at Vizcaya one Sunday afternoon in December 1992. The wealthy Middle Eastern bride—whose name I'll remember until I go to my grave—was Fatima, and her wedding ceremony was scheduled to start at 6 p.m. At about 3:30, my team and I were busy kicking open table legs, draping chairs with custom covers, and setting tables, when I noticed a commotion around the bridal planning pioneer of those days, Lois Beinhorn.

Lois was the first planner I ever worked with. Today, anyone who plans their sister's wedding claims to be a planner. But Lois was a true professional.

Curious, I approached Lois and asked what was going on.

"Bill, you'll never believe it," she said. "The bride was getting her final coifs at a downtown Miami hair salon, and when she went to get into her car parked on the street, she discovered a broken window. Her perfectly pressed Vera Wang gown was gone!"

Someone had stolen the bride's dress just three hours before her walk down the aisle.

Even back then we had large, clunky mobile devices, and Lois's phone was blowing up with frantic calls from our distressed bride. Where could she find a new dress at this late hour?

By this time on Sundays, the Miracle Mile boutiques in Coral Gables were closed, but Lois had a solution. She flipped through her Rolodex filled with home phone numbers for her vendors and quickly roused one of the bridal salon owners, who was resting at home. The owner raced 10 miles to her store to outfit the panicky bride with a new dress.

Fatima was a perfect size two, so few alterations were needed, but obviously she was going to be late to her own wedding.

Meanwhile, back at Vizcaya, guests were beginning to arrive—and the pressure was mounting. What should we do? What *could* we do?

My aim is to delight my guests, not distress them, so my team and I jumped into overdrive, opening the bars an hour earlier than planned. I directed the kitchen to start passing hors d'oeuvres to the confused guests, who were wondering when the ceremony would start.

"Why are we eating and drinking now?" I heard a few ask.

As word of the stolen dress spread quickly among the guests, my team and I did our best to keep them happy—even though we weren't scheduled to start serving until after the ceremony. One of my company's mantras paid off that day—be ready for an event an hour early.

About an hour later, Fatima arrived in her beautiful new dress, and soon the ceremony began. The guests, fueled by pre-ceremony cocktails, were in great moods.

With the knot tied, we began dinner pretty much on time, with plenty of time left for toasting, cake-cutting, and—of course—dancing to the beat of a 10-piece band.

At evening's end, Lois grabbed the cake top, the cake-cutting utensils, and the toasting goblets as the happy couple slipped into the back of an awaiting stretch limo to be whisked away to the Grand Bay Hotel some two miles away, where they would spend their wedding night before jetting off on their honeymoon.

Fast-forward to the next morning, when who should show up at my office but the bride's brother, looking for lost-and-found items like jewelry, disposable cameras, and even a missing shoe or two.

We're not responsible for lost items, but we retrieve whatever we can at the end of each event, particularly scouting the area for glassware that may have been left out of sight. For every missing item, the rental firm charges three times the original cost, so we search high and low for hidden items. And, yes, we find other things, too—some unmentionable.

I gave the bride's brother what we found, and then asked, "Did they find the person who stole your sister's wedding dress?"

"Yes, Bill, we did." It was the groom's former girlfriend.

I thought to myself, *How mean can you be? Get over it, girl.*

While I've never heard of this scenario happening to anyone else, it proves the adage: If it can go wrong, it will.

Not only do successful business teams—like mine and Lois's—have to expect the unexpected, but we must also go above and beyond what's expected to make sure our clients are happy. We weren't responsible for the stolen wedding dress, but we made sure our clients were happy despite the near disaster. Lois took care of the bride while we took care of the waiting guests.

We all only have one chance to get it right.

MAKE YOUR CLIENTS FEEL VALUED

When an architectural company in Miami wanted to host a cocktail reception celebrating their 25th anniversary, they hired my friend Gladys Mezrahi, president and CEO of Miami's Indigo Events.

Gladys—who's created intricate international events for major corporations—could plan a cocktail party in her sleep. But she delved deeper, asking a question she poses to all her clients: "What is your real objective?" Turns out, the company wanted to win back some major clients it had lost after a change in leadership and hoped inviting them to the anniversary celebration would seal the deal.

"A cocktail reception isn't going to cut it," Gladys advised her client. The head of the company or key decision-maker most likely wouldn't even show up to the party. At best, they might send a congratulatory bouquet. Her client needed to offer something much more personal to get the companies' attention.

So Gladys came up with the idea of hosting an individual lunch or dinner for each of the 10 companies her client was wooing. She worked with an executive assistant at each firm to make sure that key executives would be available on the date chosen, and that it would be in a convenient location that would be a draw. The messaging changed, too. Instead of inviting each former client to share in their anniversary celebration, the architecture firm was thanking each one individually for the role it had played in their success. The events became about the customers the company wanted to win back.

Making their former customers feel valued paid off for the architecture firm. Six of the 10 hired Gladys's client for more projects.

As Gladys understands, if you're a business owner, you're in the business of relationships. You can only build a relationship by providing good service—and you can only build a great relationship by providing great service.

Think about your favorite companies. Why are you loyal to them? Often, you'll choose one company over another because their service feels personalized. My co-author Sara is a big fan of Chewy, the online pet supply company, for its fast shipping and wide selection. She became a bigger Chewy fan when she started receiving annual birthday cards from the company for her cats, Mookie and Misha. The cards make her laugh, remind her of her cats' birthdays, and strengthen her relationship with the brand.

One of my role models, Chuck Mercurio, demonstrated the power of relationships when he was the director of catering at the Sheraton River House in the 1980s. The hotel's location didn't sell itself. It was a corporate, commercial airport hotel that you had to go through a warehouse district to find. And yet, under Chuck's leadership, there were 145 major social functions happening at the hotel every year, raking in $1.5 million—and that's in the '80s!

I asked Chuck how he managed to pull this off in South Florida, where the competition is fierce—and many hotels have enviable beachfront locations. "It just so happened that through the years I had developed good relationships with the rabbis and/or members of the congregations of five Jewish temples in South Miami and Kendall, which produced just one referral after another," he said.

Plus, the hotel hosted many baby showers and engagement parties for the Cuban community. "So much was brought in by one particular bride-to-be that we did her engagement party for free as a thank you," added Chuck. In other words, Chuck made strong connections with people—and those connections paid off time and time again.

BE THERE WHEN YOUR CLIENTS ARE READY

Tech-savvy millennials are a high-spending and high-earning generation. They also have a mantra, according to author and speaker T. Scott Gross: "My way, right away, why pay?"

In other words, millennials want quick, customizable service that is negotiated on their terms and delivers great value. And when millennials want help, they want it now; when they don't want help, they expect the sales staff to be invisible. Therefore, being the "first mover" to serve your clients at the time they wish to be served exponentially improves your chances to serve them well. When you do this, they will pay a fair price.

Put yourself in the shoes of your typical client. When you go to make a major purchase, do you do it immediately? Probably not. And as you shop for a major purchase—such as a car, house, or even a wedding reception—are there times when you're ready to buy and other times when you're just looking?

Of course. Yet when your customer takes that first proactive step toward purchasing with an initial inquiry, you'll increase your chance to close the deal with a speedy text, call, email, or live chat. Delta Air Lines understood the first-mover advantage with its old ad slogan: Delta Is Ready When You Are.

Some say there are advantages to not being available all the time. In fact, one of my mentors—Mike Roman, the founder of Catersource—once said, "The best caterers play hard to get."

That may be true if you're dealing with ultra-luxury clients. Appearing so in-demand that your time for potential new clients is limited may boost your cachet. However, you'll also be limiting the number of clients that you can serve.

My concierge service is available to all people planning an event—whether it's a backyard party and they need one bartender, or it's a lavish society gala at Miami's Vizcaya Museum and Gardens and they need all the help money can buy.

You only have seconds to keep the attention of a shopper. Some say seven. Many people have the attention spans of gnats and will quickly fly away.

So we do our best to be like Delta ... ready when our clients are ready. We have used live chat, and sales team members answer the phone during normal business hours, and return calls on nights and weekends, when couples have time to plan their events. And I personally love to respond to client inquiries ... in fact, just before writing this, I responded to a lead for catering for Miami Swim Week.

"Why pay?" is the other part of the millennial mantra. Most shoppers are looking for a deal, a bargain, or something unique. With technology, it's easy to shop prices online if you're looking for a specific product.

However, some products are harder to quantify—like catering, with its nuances of service, food quality and presentation, and location. Serving the same meal to a group in a high-rise office building will be considerably more costly than serving it in a restaurant with a private room, thanks to the logistics involved.

But here's the key: Clients are willing to pay more for hand-holding service—particularly couples planning their once-in-a-lifetime wedding. To capture the millennial dollar, however, you need to prove to them that you're offering services they can't get elsewhere.

When Southern Way Catering in Columbia, South Carolina, found itself receiving poor service from a party rental company, it decided to beat the firm at their own game—and won.

For years, Southern Way was the biggest customer of the firm and was treated accordingly. "We were accustomed to being treated like the best client and getting what we needed when we needed it," says Jesse Bullard, Southern Way's vice president. The rental company was ready to serve Southern Way when Southern Way was ready to be served. Yet after the rental firm was purchased by a much larger company, prices increased—and service took a nosedive.

When Jesse complained, the new owner replied, "You just have to get used to it."

Instead, Southern Way launched its own rental company, focusing exclusively on renting to other businesses in the hospitality industry rather than consumers. Six years later, Southern Way's party rental firm is doing exceptionally well, and is widely known as the leader in its market.

"We're actually more expensive than they are, and they have more inventory than us, but we've competed on service," says Jesse. "You can have the best food in the world, the prettiest tablecloths in the world, the nicest china, the biggest tents, the shiniest trucks, but you still have got to have great service. It is people that this whole industry revolves around."

DON'T LET HIGH TECH GET IN THE WAY OF HIGH TOUCH

High-tech solutions allow us to create more opportunities for high-touch service. As a huge fan of Facebook and LinkedIn, I use these technologies to learn more about my clients and prospects. People are impressed when you have taken the time to learn more about them. Some say it's stalking … I say it's finding connections so we can better understand and serve our customers.

Another high-tech solution we use is a software program called Tripleseat. Costing one-quarter of the price of Salesforce, it's the perfect solution for caterers, as well as restaurant owners and operators. It streamlines the booking process by quickly creating professional proposals and is a foolproof system for helping to manage events, tracking sales, leads, and guest information.

While the right tech tools can save you time and money, it's a mistake to rely on them completely. Letting high tech get in the way of high touch is a recipe for failure. What are the little things you can do to show your customers you care? Once you figure that out, you'll be setting yourself apart from the competition.

In my business, when couples and corporate clients are investing huge amounts of money to create memorable experiences for their guests, they want to deal with people—not computer screens.

For many couples, their wedding is the biggest investment they've made so far, and they need to be "walked down the aisle" with someone they trust long before they actually walk down the aisle. They need to feel that someone truly understands their needs, wants, and desires.

In 2020, I came up with a way to save our clients time while showing them that we'll go above and beyond what they're paying us to do. I've witnessed so many couples squander away weeks trying to find the best vendors for their weddings—from florists and bands to venues and DJs. Meanwhile, I've lived in South Florida since 1975 so I know the territory … the good, the great, and the not-so-good venues and vendors. My staff are experts as well.

So we created a complimentary concierge service for our couples. We will point them toward the best businesses for their needs—and we have no vested interest in who they choose. Just like a hotel concierge helps you make the most of your vacation, we help our customers make the most of their weddings.

This concierge service separates my business from the competition. Ruth Stafford Peale, the wife of Norman Vincent Peale, coined the phrase, "Find a need and fill it." That's what we did—and in doing so, we help our clients feel valued.

Your customers pay everyone's wages, and when you make them feel good, they'll come back again and again—and sing your praises to friends and family.

MAKE THE RIGHT FIRST IMPRESSION

First impressions are the almost-instant conclusions we draw when meeting someone for the first time. We form this opinion by quickly taking in information about a person, including his or her face, dress, posture, and tone of voice. And the first seven seconds of an interaction can make or break your chances to win that person's business.

Have you ever walked into a business for an appointment, and there's no one there to greet you? You either wait at the desk or poke around the area, searching for a person to talk to. With each second that passes, that business falls farther and farther behind in its chances to make a good impression.

We faced a dilemma at our popular wedding venue, Villa Woodbine in Coconut Grove. The mansion sits at the end of a long driveway, with the entrance at the rear of the property. Our offices are upstairs on the second floor. Since our layout prohibits a reception desk, how can we make a good first impression?

Here's what we came up with: We ask our clients to text us when they're five minutes away. Then a staff member waits at the door, greeting the visitor upon arrival—either at the door or in the parking lot.

I'll never forget the time a highly respected South Florida caterer invited me to visit him at his home to review his forthcoming book. He had done his homework and knew that I love cashews. When we sat down, there was a bowl of those luscious nuts in front of me on the coffee table. How do you think that meeting went?

Of course, a warm smile and eye contact are givens when you meet someone.

But don't forget professional attire, grooming, posture, and punctuality. Here in Miami, people are not known for being on time. So we stress punctuality in our training. In fact, we have a mantra—"If you're on time, you're late!"

There are exceptions, however. In my salad days of catering, I would take a six-mile run mid-afternoon and return an hour or so later, shirtless, soaking in sweat, and gasping for breath. One particularly hot and muggy summer day, a mom and her daughter were waiting for me upon my return. I'd forgotten our appointment. Somehow, I was able to apologize and charm them into booking their Vizcaya wedding. I was transparent and authentic, and put myself in their shoes … they had waited in the sun, so I immediately brought them inside for some ice-cold water (for them and for me!).

Here's another trick of the trade—find something in common! If you're not a natural chit-chatter, like I am—which usually leads to discovering mutual connections—do your homework in advance. Never go into a first meeting cold. Go online and learn something about the person you're meeting with. It's research that will pay off in spades.

Or, when you're arranging the meeting, ask a few questions and take notes—find out things like alma maters, children, hobbies, pets. Then mention those things at your first meeting. You'll impress your client by showing that you were listening, making them feel important. And isn't that what we all want?

GIVE THEM WHAT THEY NEED … AND SOME EXTRA FOR GOOD MEASURE

Going that extra mile serving your clients leaves them with fond memories—and increases the likelihood for return business.

Doing more than what is expected cements your service in the minds of your clients. In catering, one of the more difficult tasks is after-dinner tableside coffee service. It requires trained staff to juggle guests who wish to have coffee—regular or decaf—and those tea drinkers who many times are the last to be served.

If you're a tea drinker, you know what I mean. Service trainer Ian Maksik used to say tea drinkers need to bring their own tea bags, lemon wedges, and knee pads so they can get down on their knees and beg a server for a cup of hot water.

Now for that extra touch to solve the coffee drinker dilemma. The late, great caterer Michael Pecora, owner of Signature Grand and Signature Gardens in Miami, resolved the issue of tableside coffee service. His secret was offering a complimentary Irish coffee station, with large bowls of whipped cream and plenty of Irish whiskey. It only required one staff member to service the table. And even though guests had to get their own coffee, they were delighted when they realized they could add a free tipple to their brew.

In catering, the serving of the entrée is another potential minefield. If you've ever sat and waited … and waited … for your meal after your salad plate was cleared, it's not your server's fault; there's a bottleneck in the kitchen. In a genius maneuver, Michael moved the kitchen to the dining area on movable buffet lines, announcing their entry with music, lighting, and even smoke. That might sound corny today, but it worked.

One by one, servers would approach these movable feasts with one plate in each hand. The culinary team would dish up the main course onto the waiting plates, and like an army the servers would sweep the room, serving food extremely hot and fresh as the banquet captain directed traffic to ensure that everyone was served in order.

Michael not only made sure customers were happy, he entertained them in the process—adding something extra.

The Ritz-Carlton hotel brand is known for going the extra mile. Horst Schulze, Ritz-Carlton's cofounder, gave an example of how the luxury hotel chain earned that reputation in a post on *CustomerThink*. As Schulze wrote, a guest at the hotel accidentally left his laptop in the room when he checked out. He flew to Hawaii and called the hotel, panicking because he needed that computer for a meeting. The housekeeper who found the laptop was empowered to do what was necessary to take care of this guest: She took the very next flight to Hawaii, returned the computer to the guest, and took the next flight back to the mainland.

Everyone wants to feel important, accepted, and appreciated. A colleague in the restaurant business—John Offerdahl, a former Miami Dolphins football star—gives 100 percent of his attention to each customer. When we met for coffee a few years ago, he maintained great eye contact and asked question after question about me and my life. How do you think that made me feel? I'm a customer for life ... and the other staff members at his restaurant follow his lead, making each customer feel like an audience of one.

Of course, every business will fail to live up to expectations from time to time. Some will do no service recovery and lose the customer. Others will offer a credit or a refund, while those that go the extra mile will gain a loyal customer.

For example, if a customer complains your coffee isn't hot enough, do more than just refund the price of that cup. Offer a complimentary cup of coffee every day for a month. Once that customer walks back through the door for the free coffee, he or she is sure to buy something else ... and your generosity will earn their loyalty.

ANTICIPATE CUSTOMERS' NEEDS

How many times have you been served coffee with no cream or sugar? Or a burger without ketchup or mustard? Great service providers always include such commonly requested extras because they put themselves in their customers' shoes, understanding what they need before they can even ask.

Hilton CEO Chris Nassetta loves listening to music when he travels, so he carries a Bose micro speaker with him in his briefcase. Realizing that many Hilton guests also like to play their favorite tunes while on the road, he suggested that Hilton's Tempo brand include a Bluetooth speaker in each guest bathroom mirror. The incremental cost is just $15 per room, he noted, but the small expense pays off in guest satisfaction. Travelers like having the technology at their fingertips without the hassle of remembering to pack an extra gadget.

Successful service providers think through the guest experience, imagining what might cause stress or concern, and find ways to alleviate those issues before they can occur. For example, when John Bach was coming up with the services he would offer at his successful Los Angeles catering company—Seoul Food Korean BBQ—he knew he wanted to give guests a taste of what they'd experience at a traditional Korean barbecue restaurant, where diners cook their own meat on a grill in the middle of the table. He realized, however, that not all guests would be comfortable with that concept.

"It can be very intimidating for people, because it's a new way of eating," says John. "So we handle it for them so it's a comfortable experience." When guests book Seoul Food's popular Signature Service, they'll dine at a table outfitted with camp stoves topped with cast aluminum pans. However, John or one of his chefs will be cooking the meats, serving them directly from the grill to the plates, while chatting with guests and explaining each dish. With their own tongs, guests can try grilling their own meats if they'd like—but only if they want to.

In the event catering business, anticipating the customer's needs starts with valet parking. No one wants to wait in a long line of cars before entering the venue. Clients don't foresee this type of issue, so by offering sufficient valet staff and parking, this first potential problem at a wedding or event is headed off at the pass.

After the drive, guests are thirsty and hungry. So we always serve a passed welcome drink as well as some small bites prior to dinner or the wedding ceremony.

My team and I are far from perfect, and always striving to improve. While writing this section of the book, I received an email from a client who was not pleased with the house wine served at her event. Of course, the wine we served was listed in our contract, but we dropped the ball by not digging deeper into this customer's likes and dislikes. Had we done that and learned that she and her guests were "into" wine, we could have offered better selections—and considerably increased our check average and gross margins.

In all industries, those companies that anticipate customers' needs before they ask are way ahead of the game when it comes to customer loyalty. Shopping on Amazon is a great example—if you've searched for something, that search will appear next time you log on, along with items you've bought before and similar products. Amazon knows what you need before you do!

Anticipating your customers' needs can get trickier over time. According to Microsoft's Global State of Customer Service report in 2020, 55 percent of customers expect better customer service year over year. In other words, their expectations are higher—so your service levels must be, too. Hubspot's Annual State of Service Report shows even greater numbers: 88 percent of respondents agreed that customers have higher expectations than in the past, and 79 percent said customers are smarter and more informed.

Customers desire frictionless experiences with no hassles. And the best way to find out what they expect is to ask them. Jug-eared Ross Perot used to joke, "I'm all ears!" Be all ears when you're communicating with your customers.

Consider asking your customers to take a brief survey with questions such as these:

- Tell us how you like working with us.
- Is there anything you would like to change about our relationship?
- What should my firm be doing more of? Less of?
- How would you rate the communications between you and my team?
- What have we done to be most helpful to your business?
- How can we make your life easier?
- How can we make doing business with us easier?
- How can we improve our listening skills to meet your needs?

When you get the answers to these questions, pull a Ross Perot—listen! Take your customers' answers and devise ways for you and your team to better anticipate their needs—thereby increasing your revenue, margins, and bottom-line profits.

GIVE YOUR CLIENTS PEACE OF MIND

One of my biggest inspirations, the legendary Zig Ziglar, said, "Everybody wants the same things—to be happy, to be healthy, to be at least reasonably prosperous, and to be secure. They want friends, peace of mind, good family relationships, and hope that tomorrow is going to be even better than today."

My team and I sell catering and event services, but what we really sell is peace of mind. Clients trust us to deliver legendary service to delight their guests. That isn't their job; it's our job. And they shouldn't have to worry that we won't deliver.

Selling peace of mind for wedding couples and their families is tricky due to the emotions involved. Most couples lack knowledge about what they need. They may have never bought catering before, and after the engagement rush wears off, there's a reality check—they realize they need to plan and pay for something they've never had to plan or pay for before. And on the big day, all their closest friends and relatives will be there to witness any potential problems.

Plus, wedding planning can be long and complicated, involving several events and vendors—there's the rehearsal dinner, the ceremony, the reception, guest accommodations, transportation, gifts for the wedding party … on and on it goes. Since top venues like Villa Woodbine book two years in advance, the planning process is drawn out, providing plenty of opportunities for conflict and pitfalls.

At Bill Hansen Catering, we help wedding clients have peace of mind by serving as counselors. For example, we encourage couples to assemble the guest list *together*. Since the "b" word—budget—can be contentious, we ask couples to rank expenses—including food, beverages, music, photography, and more—from most important to least important. Since most couples can't afford the best in all categories, this helps them to clarify their priorities and keep the peace.

We also advise couples to celebrate when they check things off their planning lists, and to create "wedding-free" zones, where they're not allowed to talk about anything wedding-related.

Here's a lesson that I took to heart from the Sales Gravy training platform: Peace of mind may be hard to define, but we know it when we experience it. It's the hidden benefit that everyone wants when buying.

People gravitate toward their favorite airlines, hotels, restaurants, grocery stores, pharmacies, and car brands because they know what to expect. In these cases, familiarity doesn't breed contempt; it breeds contentment.

PAY ATTENTION TO DETAIL

While an officer in the U.S. Navy, I learned to pay attention to detail—something the U.S. military has down to a science. For example, if a superior found a loose thread on your uniform—known as "Irish pennants"—you'd get a "red gig." Once those red gigs reached a certain number, you'd receive a disciplinary action.

Pay attention to the loose threads in your business.

Here's a story I like to share when speaking to a group of students. I ask for a show of hands when I ask this series of questions:

How many of you have been bitten by a mosquito? All hands go up.

What about a no-see-um? Most hands go up.

A gnat? Most hands again.

A bee, hornet, or wasp? Some hands go up.

What about an elephant? How many of you have been bitten by an elephant? Obviously, no one raises a hand.

Remember, I say, *it's the little things that will bite you in this business.*

In any industry, it's the little things that separate the stars from the amateurs. Cleanliness is the first sign a company pays attention to detail—and I'm not just talking about physical cleanliness. An online presence with poor design, uninspiring images, and typos makes a poor first impression.

In my business, great table service reflects lots of attention to detail—for example, when a server notices a client is left-handed and places the coffee cup to the left of the customer with the handle at eight o'clock. We also train our table servers to ensure:

- Salt and pepper shakers are filled to the brim and grease-free.
- Uniforms are clean and crisp.
- Menus are clean.
- Tables are level.
- Tabletops are picture-perfect, with pressed linens.
- Food is consistently served from one side and cleared from the other.
- They're making eye contact and smiling when interacting with guests.
- They're knowledgeable about the menu.
- They thank guests as they leave.

I have two modes of operation—Big Picture Bill and Nit-Picky Bill. I can do both, but I'm much more of a big picture guy.

For the nit-picky stuff that you must get done, here are some pointers:

- Do your detail work when you can focus without interruptions.
- Double- and triple-check your work.
- Ask others to check and review your work. I'm a quick writer and can easily share my general ideas; however, I do not have the patience to check for grammar, editing, and proofreading. I leave those tasks to my co-author, Sara.

- Make sure you're well-staffed so details don't get overlooked—little things slip through the cracks if your team is understaffed and overworked.

And remember the story of the elephant and the insects. It's the little things that will come back to bite you.

INDULGE ALL THE SENSES

People eat with their eyes. If the tastiest dish in the world looks like a blob on a plate, who's going to try it? At my company, we aim to create experiences that touch hearts, minds, and souls through sensory experiences of taste, smell, sound, touch, and—of course—sight.

Start with the basics. When couples come to us to plan their weddings, most are as nervous as a long-tailed cat in a room full of rocking chairs. So we speak to them in soothing, assured voices, calming their nerves.

Offer customers a hot or cold beverage. Serve snacks that fill the air with a pleasant aroma, like freshly baked cinnamon buns or chocolate-chip cookies.

Think about your favorite hotel and why you like it. You probably feel more relaxed from the moment you enter the lobby. Successful hotels aim to engage the senses, with many creating signature scents that waft through the properties. If you're a fan of the W Hotels chain, for example, you may have purchased its citrusy room spray to recreate in your own home the calming atmosphere you enjoy as a guest.

Background music to fit the mood can turn shoppers into eager buyers. According to branding expert Martin Lindstrom—author of *Brand Sense: Sensory Secrets Behind the Stuff We Buy*—"brands with music that 'fit' their brand identity are 96 percent likelier to prompt memory recall."

In fact, sensory input can affect buying decisions without customers even realizing it. A study in 1999 published in the *Journal of Applied Psychology* found that playing French-style music in a wine shop led to customers purchasing more French wine, and the same correlation was found between German music and German wine. However, when asked about the music's impact on their purchases, customers said they didn't notice the music or its effect. It worked subconsciously.

If you're married, you may have gone to tastings at different catering companies to try their food and choose what to serve to your wedding guests. Do you remember much about those tastings? Probably not, as for many it's just one more item to check off a to-do list before the big day. At Bill Hansen Catering, we wanted to change that.

In June 2024, we hosted our first Date Night—an invitation-only, immersive event for engaged couples who had either booked or were considering booking their wedding reception at Villa Woodbine or one of our preferred venues. Guests experienced what it would be like to have their wedding at our romantic venue, with a jazz saxophonist playing, carbon dioxide bubbles floating through the air, and welcoming flutes of champagne. The couples tasted a variety of hors d'oeuvres and signature drinks during the cocktail hour before enjoying a sample dinner menu curated from each of their choices. Our cake vendors then invited the guests to try their flavors and see their creative designs.

The feedback was off the charts. An Instagram reel of Date Night racked up 14,000 views in a week. Plus, believe it or not, the cost per couple for this memorable night was less than it would have been for a standard individual tasting.

Working with our vendors, we created a magical night for these couples that indulged all the senses. We made our clients feel special—and we were able to upsell by demonstrating all the extras that couples could add to their wedding celebrations.

My friend Meryl Snow tells a story about how emotions influence buying decisions. Meryl cofounded Feastivities Events in Philadelphia and shares her sales expertise with others through her consulting firm, SnowStorm Solutions. One day, Meryl was strolling through Nordstrom on her way to the mall when a red dress caught her eye. "I made a beeline over there and just fell in love with it—it was so me!" recalls Meryl. Once she saw the $650 price tag, however, she reluctantly put the dress back on the rack.

As she was leaving the mall, Meryl passed the red dress again—and couldn't resist trying it on. "The dress looked amazing! It fit me perfectly," she remembers. "I felt that it complemented my coloring and made me look slim. I just had to have it!" After buying the dress, Meryl wondered, "What just happened? How did I go from thinking the dress was too expensive to excitedly buying it?"

Meryl realized she bought the dress *because of how it made her feel*. When you can tap into someone's emotions, you're much more likely to seal the deal.

AFTER DROPPING THE BALL, MAKE A SWIFT RECOVERY

Service recovery has proven to be one of the best tools for retaining clients. No one is perfect. Off-premise catering is a recipe for myriad potential disasters that need to be resolved in an instant, before the client discovers the miscue.

But what happens when we fail to resolve an issue, and we receive a legitimate complaint about something that headed south at a wedding or event? We figure out a way to make it up to them.

Years ago, before the days of mobile phones, we forgot to show up to cater a rehearsal dinner on a yacht. Fortunately, the client was able to scramble for some food before sailing. While that was a big mistake, we earned back the client's trust by catering a complimentary Sunday brunch for the group at the Miami Beach Golf Course two days later. It worked—the client and his wife are dear friends of ours to this day.

From time to time, we've offered refunds when the client wasn't pleased with the level of service they received. Sometimes it was our fault, and other times the client failed to communicate what they needed—and we failed to be persistent and ask for it.

Despite these setbacks, we continue to be by far the most trusted catering brand in South Florida—44-plus years in business means we are who we say we are.

When faced with a complaining customer, put your ego on the shelf. Be humble and listen. Yes, it's your business, and it's part of you, but this is not the time to puff out your chest about all your successes. Remember—many of your successes are thanks to changes you made after customer feedback.

Thank them for sharing their displeasure with you, then listen with focus and intent. Take notes and ask questions if you don't understand something. Be kind, with the intention of earning back your customer's trust.

Email is OK, but a face-to-face meeting or video conferencing allows you to convey emotions and non-verbal cues. This is a nice way to show that you really intend to help and solve the problem that led to the complaint.

And before you decide what to do about the situation, repeat what you heard the customer say—and get their buy-in for the solution you come up with.

This is when the rubber meets the road. How will you fix the problem? Here are some steps I've taken with unhappy customers over the years:

- First, offer a partial refund or a credit toward a future event.
- Then send a thank you gift for bringing the issue to your attention.
- Finally, follow up to ensure you've regained the customer's trust and future business.

Make sure to document the complaints and share them with your team, coming up with solutions so they won't happen again.

CHAPTER 3
RISK-TAKING
A TURTLE GOES NOWHERE UNTIL IT STICKS ITS NECK OUT

Recently, armed with COVID relief money, I invested in a couple of businesses—both risky, both mistakes. They were not sure things, nor did I have the bandwidth to manage them well, giving the reins to others. Big mistake.

Hindsight is clearer than foresight, but I realize now that I should have involved the team from my mothership and very profitable Bill Hansen Catering. Live and learn.

If you never venture into the unknown, however, you'll never grow beyond your current borders, as I've discovered time and time again. Just make sure to analyze the risks and consider the worst-case scenario.

GET OUT OF YOUR COMFORT ZONE AND INTO YOUR CHALLENGE ZONE

My team members sometimes call me "The Cowboy," since I'm known for riding out onto the range, lassoing new opportunities—without first considering the risks and getting a posse behind me.

While due diligence is often wise, there are times when you must go with your gut and take a gamble. The payoff can be huge.

In December 1982, I stumbled upon a forlorn villa in Miami that turned into one of my biggest jackpots.

The adventure started when a medical group from a local hospital reached out to me to find a venue for their holiday party on the second Saturday of December. In the catering world, this is one of the most sought-after dates of the year. Yet I managed to secure them a unique venue—Villa Serena, a bayfront mansion on Brickell Avenue, two miles south of downtown Miami.

Built in 1913, Villa Serena was the winter home of famed three-time presidential candidate William Jennings Bryan. The Bryans hosted many important events and social gatherings at the estate.

I was as excited as my clients about the venue since its privacy and exclusivity were unparalleled at the time. The owner's daughter, Theresa Nagymihaly Rust, gave me the go-ahead to start planning … and I did. But I didn't plan on receiving her phone call 10 days before the event, advising me there'd been a tragedy at the home, and my event was off. I never found out what the tragedy was.

In those days, I was greener than a bell pepper in the off-premise catering world. I didn't have a contract or a deposit. So, I was up the proverbial creek.

I embraced the challenge, however. After giving my clients the bad news, I searched for another historic venue in that area. The easy road would have been to say, "I'm sorry things didn't work out," and move on. But that's never been the way I operate.

A business group colleague told me about a home on South Bayshore Drive across from Kennedy Park in Coconut Grove. I called, but no one answered, so off I went to scout it in person. I was leaving my comfort zone—showing up unannounced at someone's home.

Beneath dark and stormy skies, the mansion looked like it was rumored to be—haunted. I cautiously approached the imposing wooden door and banged the wrought-iron knocker.

The door suddenly opened, and I jumped into action despite my trepidation. "I understand you rent your property out for events. Is the second Saturday in December available?" I asked the occupant.

The man didn't hesitate with his response: "No way."

Dejected, I turned to leave. But I was surprised to see someone else at the property—a stoned-out hippie peering at me from the kitchen door next to the open courtyard. Haunted house indeed.

Eventually, I found my clients a venue in the Grove Isle condominium, and they were pleased. But I couldn't stop thinking about that run-down Mediterranean manse—Villa Woodbine.

So I kept digging, determined to find out more about Villa Woodbine's inhabitants. Turns out, the stoned hippie was the lessee of the property. As luck would have it, he was about to move out to go to rehab in Atlanta. I tracked down the owner and realtor, and on another rainy day, in January 1983, I ran the four miles from downtown Miami to meet them at the villa.

In Miami, anything below 70°F is bone-chillingly cold, so we talked terms in front of the living room fireplace.

And that's when I leaped out of my comfort zone and made the move that's paying off to this day. I signed a lease on the spot, and shortly thereafter moved into the mansion with my wife, Sugar Girl, and my son Jimmy. We lived above the store, and Villa Woodbine became an events venue one or two nights a week. Or, as we liked to say, that's when we had 100 or so of our closest personal friends over for dinner.

But before we invited wedding guests into our home, we needed to clean things up. Villa Woodbine was in rough shape and even had a floor safe where the prior occupants kept their illegal substances. They left none behind (thank you for that).

Designed by architect Walter De Garmo in 1930, Villa Woodbine takes full advantage of Miami's warm tropical breezes, with open-air courtyards and large loggias framed by Spanish arches. The villa was originally built as the winter residence of Mr. and Mrs. Charles Boyd, owners of the Appleton Coated Paper Company in Wisconsin. Upon Mr. Boyd's passing in 1954, his daughter Martha and son-in-law Bill Siekman inherited the four-acre estate.

The Siekmans continued to use the home as their winter residence until the late 1950s, when their children's schooling made it impossible to spend their winters away. Then they began leasing the property to others.

Can you imagine their surprise in 1961 when, while flipping through *Life* magazine in their Appleton mansion, they saw a photo of their Miami villa, described (correctly) as the home in which the Bay of Pigs invasion was planned?

A host of colorful lessees ensued—from an architect who filled the courtyard with parrots to dreamers like treasure hunter Mel Fisher. Guests included the Village People, Mary Wilson of The Supremes, and Luciano Pavarotti. If Villa Woodbine's walls could talk ...

Although I never had the foresight to buy the property—and I don't live there anymore—my company still leases Villa Woodbine, paying 20 times more than the original lease. We've transformed the mansion into the most in-demand wedding venue in South Florida. And recently we were featured in the *Miami Herald* as Miami's best wedding venue.

Moving from my comfort zone into my challenge zone has paid off a thousand times over.

WHEN YOU STICK YOUR HEAD OUT, TAKE A GOOD LOOK AROUND

I named this chapter after one of my favorite sayings: A turtle goes nowhere until it sticks its neck out. Ironically, I once stuck my neck out *because* of a turtle—actually, a beach where turtles nested—and I failed miserably because I didn't take a good look around after I ventured from my shell.

The opportunity I thought of as "can't-miss" was on a pristine beach in a state park just south of Fort Lauderdale. The contract was for the park's concessions, which included a quaint snack bar, the Loggerhead Café—named after the turtles that nest on the beach. The deal came with plenty of business already booked and assets like a beachfront tent, a reefer truck, a house trailer for the manager, a Kubota Tractor for driving up and down the beach, kayaks, canoes, and a food-and-beverage license. The teenage Beach Boys fan in me envisioned fun, fun, fun in the sun—large catered events up and down the shoreline, with profits rolling in like the tide.

Boy, was I wrong. I'd walk away three years later, two years before my contract expired, wishing I'd never stuck my neck out.

The gleaming white sand blinded me to the venture's downsides. I wanted in so badly that I took the seller at his word. He said there was no need to worry about the rules against selling and serving alcohol on the beach … officials turned a blind eye, he assured me. And, yes, protected turtles nested on the beach, but that wouldn't affect my operations.

Like a fool, I failed to investigate these matters myself. It wasn't long before I was summoned to the park manager's office so he could rattle off a list of complaints against me. Seems I wasn't observing the rules regarding turtle-friendly lights on the beach, which made it virtually impossible to host nighttime events for two-thirds of the year (bright lights can deter female turtles from nesting and disorient hatchlings as they try to venture seaward).

On top of that, the alcohol rules *were* strictly enforced. Until sundown, alcohol could not be served on the beach, only at the snack bar—which, by the way, had to be open 365 days a year. It wasn't easy finding staffers to work on Christmas.

Roadblock after roadblock after roadblock. Yes, there were some benefits, in the form of learning experiences. I became good friends with one of the park rangers, and one of my team members stuck with me and continues to work with me as an event manager going on 20 years.

The lesson is: Do your due diligence. Perform an audit of the company you're acquiring or doing significant business with. This audit should include financial implications, tax consequences, operational considerations, and legal ramifications. In my case at the beach, I did a great job on three out of four, but dropped the ball on the operational part, failing to review and understand the park rules.

I also neglected to seek wise counsel from others before taking the plunge. And while I learned some lessons, this would not be my last risky investment.

KNOW YOUR WEAKNESSES, STRENGTHS, AND TOLERANCE FOR RISK

I have a high tolerance for risk, and that has led to me becoming a catering and events force in South Florida. Fortunately, I've won more of my gambles than I've lost. But you must know yourself before you take big chances.

Rachael Volz, owner and CEO of A Fare Extraordinaire in Houston, knew this about herself when she embarked on a journey to convert a 1942 munitions factory into a five-star, 58,000-square-foot event space, The Revaire: "I'm a very positive person, and I really don't focus on the negative."

That attitude kept Rachael going when she ran into inevitable roadblocks. The night before The Revaire's first event, for example, the Mercury Chamber Orchestra was in the venue, practicing for a performance the following evening. The problem? It was hot as Hades.

"The musicians were sweating because the air conditioning wasn't working and it was May in Houston," says Rachael. "I didn't realize it would take two weeks for the air conditioning to properly cool the building due to the complicated control systems and the start-up staging process."

The client smiled through the rehearsal and never asked Rachael about the AC problems. The following night's benefit event, a 350-guest seated dinner, was a roaring success, and the temporary cooling units Rachael had installed kept guests cool as cucumbers. And Rachael found out why the client never batted an eye. "He was walking around with a glass of champagne telling everybody that he had bet on me, he hadn't bet on the building," she says. "And he knew that I would rather die than fail."

Rachael knew the Houston market needed a venue like The Revaire, and before purchasing the building, she projected that the earnings from her high-end catering firm would be able to pay the mortgage and build-out loans. And in the event of a dramatic reversal of wedding and events business in Houston, she still would own the real estate.

"We were in a position where we needed to make some smart investments as a family, and what better way to do that than to bet on yourself?" explains Rachael of the approach she and her husband, Jason, took. "I was naive and had no idea what was involved in a project of this size, but I believed wholeheartedly that nothing could stop me. I had a vision of the building being built and people enjoying themselves in the building, and I just visualized constantly a lot of positivity, a lot of fruitful business, a lot of peace."

Her vision materialized. The investment doubled her sales, The Revaire raised the company's profile in the luxury market, and A Fare Extraordinaire can now focus its efforts on fewer events with a higher yield.

One of my biggest sources of strength is my faith. I seek counsel from above every morning, and I can attest that when I talk to the Lord, he generally leads me to the right decisions. And when I don't take his advice, I'm in for a rough road.

My strengths also include integrity, passion, caring for others, and determination, while seeking quality in products and services.

If you're in doubt about your strengths and your weaknesses, there are numerous online tests you can take. My team recently completed the enneagram test, which helped us better understand ourselves and each other. Try it for yourself online: truity.com/test/enneagram-personality-test.

One thing I excel at is building relationships and inspiring others to be all they can be. Because of this, people flock to my doors with business opportunities. Many vie for my time and seek my treasure and talent. That's the good news.

The not-so-good news is that my success in hospitality stems from my desire to please people. That's where those in our business sometimes go astray, however. We need to be careful that we don't please others to our own detriment.

I'm somewhat of a moody person, and sometimes my emotions get the better of me. I can go orbital about a new project and the next day look at the same opportunity with gloom and doom. That's the way the Lord made me.

To balance my emotional outlook, I've learned to seek wise counsel from my team and trusted outsiders. They prevent me from pulling the trigger too soon.

According to conventional thinking, as you age you become more risk-averse. But I've always been a contrarian. My team and I are in a financial position to take larger risks in anticipation of larger gains. We know that not all deals will be ideal, but to continue growing, we need to expand our borders into new ventures.

We call my main catering business—Bill Hansen Catering—the "mothership." It generates sufficient profits to fulfill the personal needs of the team, while enabling us to reinvest into the business, and to invest in other businesses that complement the mothership. I'm blessed that my leadership team understands that I love to "ready, fire, aim," and together we can hold off firing at a deal until we have aimed at the right targets.

Surrounding yourself with those people who possess strengths to complement your weaknesses is one key to success. And more importantly, you need to put your ego on the shelf and realize that no one knows everything. Accept this, and bring on a team that are not all "yes" men and women.

IN ORDER TO INNOVATE, CALCULATE THE RISKS

Do you wish to be known for your accomplishments, or are you content blending in with the crowd? The choice is yours.

Here's the deal: You won't innovate by sticking to the status quo. Nor will you innovate if you listen to the naysayers. You need to take risks—calculated ones. A calculated risk in business is a carefully considered decision that exposes a person to a degree of personal and financial risk that is counterbalanced by a reasonable possibility of benefit.

Risky options abound in my world of hospitality. I took a huge risk when I formed Leading Caterers of America in 1995, as a network for caterers to connect with one another and with potential clients. There was nothing like it at the time. That paid off handsomely when I sold the company five years later. A year after that, when the buyer closed their doors, with cash in hand I reinvented the brand by leading catering boot camps from coast to coast. Once I tired of that, I gave the name to the industry's professional organization, Catersource, and now it's an exclusive group of the largest caterers in the country.

One of my vendors, Joseph Veneman, risked his life savings to create StaffMate, an online staffing system that boasts the most intuitive, drag-and-drop scheduling environment for kitchens, warehouses, housekeeping, sales, retail workers, and more. Now the concept seems like a no-brainer, but when Joseph came up with the idea in 2002, "people were just figuring out that the internet could be beneficial to them," he says.

A website developer at the time, Joseph heard from a caterer client—his wife's uncle—that scheduling staff for each event was a time-consuming nightmare, requiring multiple employees and seemingly endless phone calls. He thought, "I could probably fix that with the internet." So Joseph developed and fine-tuned the software while working with the uncle's company in Massachusetts as well as two catering clients in Ohio.

When he was ready to market StaffMate, he rented a booth at Catersource, the annual catering convention, where I met him and became one of his first customers. Yet he encountered a lot of pushback at first. "People would tell me, 'I can see where this would be helpful, but no one on my staff has email,'" says Joseph. With the foresight to understand that email would soon be ubiquitous, he persisted.

Now StaffMate has thousands of employees and hundreds of clients around the world, including some of the largest hotels in the U.S. And while StaffMate has several competitors, it continues to benefit from the "first-mover advantage"—which is only bestowed on those bold enough to take their big ideas, risk their time and treasure, and bring something new to market that people want to buy.

In my field, innovative caterers are changing how people think about catering. Great Performances in New York, for example, was the first caterer to own and operate an organic farm. Think about the outdated impression of catered food—rubber chicken and dried-out vegetables in chafing pans. Compare that to the farm-fresh produce served by the likes of Great Performances, which took a risk by opening the 60-acre Katchkie Farm.

Or consider Martha Stewart, who burst on the catering scene in the 1980s with innovative menus and a unique style. Her free-flowing food displays and recipes influenced every caterer in the country. Many of us jumped on board the Martha bandwagon. She took a risk and changed the way we entertain.

Have you ever heard of an events lab incubator, where hospitality students can create their own events in a classroom setting? It's a hands-on lab where students can physically create and execute a party, wedding, fundraiser, or small corporate event. I've been doing this for years to raise funds for worthwhile charities.

We have created our own 1,600-square-foot events lab on the Biscayne Bay campus of Florida International University, funded with a major gift from my company, The Hansen Group. Clearly, this is a risk of time, treasure, and talent, but it's calculated since we will discover breakthrough ways to raise the bar for entertaining. Plans include unique tabletop settings, creative cuisine, digital mapping, soundscapes, unique aromas, and virtual reality.

Yes, innovation is risky. However, the rewards can be great—and it all starts with brainstorming, a group discussion to produce ideas or solve problems. Once all the ideas are on the table, then discuss the risk/reward/feasibility.

Some brainstorming questions to ask are:

- What do our customers need that we do not supply?
- How can we meet those needs?
- How much time, treasure, and talent will it take?

Keep in mind there will always be naysayers to every idea—the energy sappers, rather than the energy givers. They may have valid points, but dwelling too much on the negative will slow the process down and lead to burnout.

GAIN A COMPETITIVE ADVANTAGE BY TAKING A RISK

When caterers are asked what their competitive advantage is, nine times out of 10 they will answer something along the lines of "great food, great service, and a great team." But is that really a competitive advantage in the eyes of a potential client? Won't your competitors be claiming the same?

Without taking risks to gain competitive advantages, businesses can grow stale, sales can stall, and attractive offers will pass you by.

Michael "Funky" Forgus discovered the importance of competitive advantages when he was considering selling his Cincinnati company, Funky's Catering, in 2010. The offer he received was laughable. Why? The buyer told him he had no protected revenue or contracts, making his company less desirable.

This wake-up call prompted Michael to build his business over the next decade. He took a risk by merging with another catering company—Vonderhaar's Catering Inc.—and taking over operations at three Cincinnati venues. Vonderhaar's and Funky's now operate under a new brand name, DelightMore, which has become the city's go-to caterer. Sales have grown exponentially. "It was the best business decision I ever made," says Michael.

A common error is to try to compete on price alone. Yet if you focus your efforts on being the low-cost choice, you can easily be undercut. In catering, mom-and-pop businesses sprout up all the time—many without licenses or insurance. Running on a shoestring, they quickly become the low-price choice. There goes your "competitive advantage."

A roofing company in Fort Lauderdale successfully shifted away from competing on price alone. Gregg Wallick, CEO of Best Roofing, describes his previous approach to sales as "bid and beg." That worked well when there was plenty of new construction—and plenty of business to go around. However, the 2008 recession brought the construction industry to a standstill. Wallick had to find a new way to attract business.

He came up with a new motto: "We Solve Roofing Problems." He positioned his company as a *problem-solver*. He's not competing on price any longer. Instead, he sells peace of mind to his customers, and that's invaluable. After differentiating his company from the competition, Best Roofing is flourishing.

At Bill Hansen Catering, we've outlined some of our competitive advantages, so we can clearly communicate them to potential clients:

- We have catered at more than 5,000 South Florida venues since 1980, which demonstrates our versatility, flexibility, and creativity.
- We have catered for more than 15,000 clients over five decades while keeping up with the latest trends.

- More than 100 of the Fortune 500 firms have experienced our professional catering.
- We are the only South Florida caterer that has catered for four U.S. presidents and Pope John Paul II. (President George H.W. Bush came back for seconds of our Oak-Grilled Duck Breast with Lychee Salsa!)
- Our staff does not accept tips during an event, other than those where we are selling food and beverages to patrons. At hosted events, you, as our client, pay a service charge for the staff.
- Our management team has 28 years of hospitality education experience at universities such as FIU and Cornell, bringing you the most professional wedding and event management in South Florida.
- Our corporate executive chef, Dewey LoSasso, has competed on the Food Network's *Chopped* and is a local celebrity.
- Our weddings have been featured in such notable publications as *Vogue, Martha Stewart Weddings, Brides,* Yahoo News, *Southern Bride, New York Post, Modern Luxury Weddings, The Knot, BizBash,* and many more.
- We train our own service staff members and rely very little on outside staffing agencies, consistently bringing you excellent service with a smile. Many team members are students and graduates of FIU's famed Chaplin School of Hospitality & Tourism Management, where CEO Bill Hansen has taught since 1990.
- Our catering services are preferred by most of the destination management companies in South Florida. These firms know our competition, and they choose us.
- Our marketing is second to none. For couples who desire national media exposure for their wedding, we're your best choice.

- In December 2023, we were voted by *Miami Herald* readers as being the Best Caterer in Miami, with Villa Woodbine voted the Best Wedding Venue.
- Bill Hansen, CEO, literally wrote the book on catering, which is used at universities around the country, including Cornell, FIU, and the University of Houston. *Off-Premise Catering Management* by Bill Hansen, published by John Wiley, is available on amazon.com.
- We understand that there's no second chance at a first impression, so we are diligent about answering phones, returning phone calls, and providing on-time proposals and proposal revisions. You won't need to call us to find out why you didn't get your proposal.
- We know the importance of first impressions for your guests as well, so we go out of our way to make sure there are no valet parking delays, that your guests are served drinks quickly without long lines at the bar, and that hors d'oeuvres are passed speedily, with one passer for every 20 guests for the first hour of most events and receptions.

Separating yourself from the competition sometimes comes with risks. In 1983, I took a huge risk to lease a historic home in Miami—and it's by far my biggest competitive advantage today. Voted as one of the 22 most romantic wedding venues in the U.S., Villa Woodbine is on the radar of most wedding couples planning weddings in South Florida. Since clients search for venues before they search for caterers, we usually show up on engaged couples' radar before the competition. And while we can't serve every interested couple at Villa Woodbine, since dates are limited, we can serve many more at the 100-plus venues where Bill Hansen Catering is a preferred caterer.

We have another competitive advantage—we are known for being a wonderful resource for couples and corporate clients searching for a unique venue that's not in a hotel, club, or restaurant, where foodservice is already available. To capitalize on this reputation, I took a risk and have invested low-six-figures in Bill Hansen Miami Venues (www.billhansenmiamivenues.com). We chose "Miami" since it's more recognizable than "South Florida," although we showcase venues from Palm Beach, Martin, Broward, and Miami-Dade counties, as well as the Florida Keys.

Sometimes, going after that competitive advantage can backfire. A competitor thought a barbecue division would work, and it failed quickly. The company failed to brand this new division with a name that would differentiate itself from the mothership brand, an upscale catering firm.

Clearly, everything we do in business presents a risk of some kind. Here are my basic rules when determining if a risk is worth taking to gain a competitive advantage:

- Don't risk more than you can afford to lose.
- Never risk a lot for a little.

What risks do you need to take to gain a competitive advantage?

GO DEEP FOR A BIGGER CATCH

There's little risk of drowning when you're fishing along the shoreline with everyone else. But angling for the big fish requires venturing out into the deep blue sea—where you'll encounter rougher waters. My fishing waters have expanded from downtown Miami to neighboring counties, and I have been offered catering opportunities in other countries. To keep fear at bay while taking a risk, I analyze the risk versus the reward (see the previous two sections for my tips).

The blue ocean strategy represents the simultaneous pursuit of high product differentiation and low cost, making the competition irrelevant. The concept comes from the book *Blue Ocean Strategy: How to Create Uncontested Market Space and Make Competition Irrelevant* by W. Chan Kim and Renée Mauborgne.

In my business, the biggest way to go deep-sea fishing is to find or build an exclusive venue where other caterers cannot cater. This eliminates the competition. My exclusive venue, Villa Woodbine, generates nearly 50 percent of my catering revenue.

Fishing in the deep waters where the big fish swim can be treacherous, since that's also where the sharks lurk. Deep-sea fishing for business deals is generally riskier than those daily deals that swim by in the shallow waters. But because there are fewer people angling in the deep-blue water than fishing from the piers, there's less competition.

And who wouldn't rather land a half-ton bluefin tuna than a sunfish or bluegill? Yes, it takes more time, treasure, and talent to land that trophy fish—but with a bigger investment comes a bigger reward.

Here's another way my firm has ventured into the deeper waters—by purchasing other catering firms, allowing us to offer four catering brands at different price points. Those looking for high-end, luxury catering—including several of Miami's billionaires—choose our original brand, Bill Hansen Catering.

At a lower price point, offering affordable luxury, is Alexander Catering. Our third brand, Eten Catering, caters to the corporate community in Broward County, including the luxury yacht industry. One top client, Feadship, is recognized as the world leader in building custom superyachts.

And finally we have Lovables Catering & Kitchen. I came to know the brand's original owners, Elizabeth and Marilyn, in 1986 when they came to me for advice. I suggested they become involved in Catersource, run by Mike Roman, the pioneer in training caterers. They became what was known at the time as "Mike Roman's groupies," and their business grew and prospered.

Pre-pandemic, Marilyn chose to retire while Elizabeth wanted to keep the company alive. We purchased Lovables, and it immediately proved to be a great investment. Then along came COVID, and with corporate business taking a nosedive, the brand struggled.

Today, however, Elizabeth and Lovables are rocking South Florida with budget-friendly catering. In December 2023, we recognized Elizabeth as our team member of the month. In fact, 2023 was a record year for Lovables.

Acquiring other companies and offering a tier of brands isn't common in my business. But you won't know if you can land the big fish unless you cast your rod. And here's the key: Don't be afraid to fail. Each failure will bring you one step closer to that big fish client, account, opportunity, adventure, or experience.

YOU'LL NEVER KNOW UNLESS YOU TRY

What is the worst thing that could happen? What's holding you back? Is it time, money, your family? The Lord gave each one of us gifts—and not using them is a recipe for failure and an unhappy life. What can you do today to begin living your life the way it's meant to be lived?

I read a book once called *Start Ugly* by David duChemin, which celebrates the messy creative process that must take place before the realization of any dream. It encourages readers to stop waiting for inspiration to strike and to just get started. Take a cue from those Nike ads—just do it!

Paralysis by analysis keeps many of us from starting something. I'm the opposite—I get started and learn as I go. I'm not afraid to try anything (as long as it's not skydiving or bungee jumping!). I've completed the New York City Marathon, conquered my fear of public speaking, driven an Indy car, and created new businesses from scratch. Did I accomplish those goals with no hitches along the way? No way.

When I started training for the marathon, I smoked Kool cigarettes by the pack and could barely make a quarter of a mile without quitting. When I started teaching and had to stand in front of a class day after day, I was so nervous that I joked that I couldn't lead a Sunday School group in silent prayer. It was nerve-wracking to hop into that Indy car at Homestead Motor Speedway for a test drive, and it's nerve-wracking to acquire companies and expand my business. I assure you, the process is far from perfect … and it's ugly at times.

We all fear the unknown and the shame of failure. And that's OK. But we'll never know if we can succeed unless we try. Here are a few tips:

- **Start small** … or start "ugly," as duChemin wrote. My first catered event for 12 guests in 1980 was clearly ugly by today's standards—we learned the hard way not to dump romaine stems down a home garbage disposal! Fortunately, our client paid the repair bill.
- **Accept that you're afraid.** Some fear is useful, as it makes you focus on the project at hand. Yes, there will be butterflies in your stomach. Accept them and concentrate on getting the butterflies all flying in the same direction to fulfill your task.
- **Focus on what you can control, not on what might happen.** Not everything is under your control. In my first catering job, I could control the quality of the food and the level of the service, but I couldn't control the weather or the guest dynamics. I concentrated my efforts on doing the best I could with what was under my control—and let go of any other worries.
- **Manage your expectations.** Did I expect that first catering gig to be enshrined in the catering hall of fame? Of course not … I simply wanted the guests to say they enjoyed the evening, the food, and the service. That was enough. Aim high, but not so high that you'll inevitably be discouraged.

So, what dream do you have that needs to become a reality? Have you been procrastinating because you're afraid of what might happen? For me, the only audience that matters is the Lord … and I know he wants me to take risks to serve others the best I can.

How about you?

CHAPTER 4
SALES AND MARKETING
IF YOU DON'T BOOK IT, YOU CAN'T COOK IT

"Are you the chef? How do you stay so skinny?"

I hear this all the time. My response? "I book it, and they cook it!"

A catering colleague was confused when I told him that I didn't cook, but that I did, on occasion, boil water. He didn't see that there's much more to catering than the food. Whatever business you're in, sales must take priority.

FIND WHAT YOU'RE BEST AT

I learned early on that my time is best spent on sales and marketing. Yes, I've helped with "plate up" and expediting, but my team knows to keep me out of the kitchen. My Nicaraguan culinary team used to tell me I make them "nerviosa" when I'm working beside them. And that's fine with me, though I will be there for them in an emergency.

If I had been the cook when I launched my business in 1980, my doors would have closed that same year. My gift is making it rain, and for nearly five decades I've done that quite well. In the early 1980s, we were one of *Inc. Magazine*'s fastest-growing small businesses. Between 2012 and 2016, we quadrupled our revenues—from $2.2 million to $8.8 million.

How did we do it? One big inspiration was Jim Collins's book *Good to Great*. Collins stresses the importance of getting the right team members on the bus and then getting them into the right seats. What influenced me the most is Collins's Hedgehog Concept, based on an ancient Greek parable, which reads: "The fox knows many things, but the hedgehog knows one big thing." Simply put, Collins encourages readers to figure out what they can be the best in the world at.

After numerous focus groups and brainstorming sessions, my team and I decided we could be the world's best catering sales and marketing organization. By following the seven strategies outlined next in this chapter, Bill Hansen Catering has become one of the top 30 catering companies in the United States, as ranked by industry publication BizBash, and the only Miami caterer included in the prestigious Leading Caterers of America organization.

SET HIGH STANDARDS AND HOLD EVERYONE ACCOUNTABLE

Sometimes, changing your perspective changes everything.

We discovered the truth of this in 2012 at Bill Hansen Catering when we changed our outlook. We stopped thinking of ourselves primarily as *caterers* and started thinking of ourselves as *marketing and sales experts* who sold catering and other services.

It all started when I got fed up with being bested by a competitor. One of my former team members was kicking my butt in the Miami catering market. I decided to start kicking back. We reorganized around this motto: "If You Don't Book It, You Can't Cook It." Sales and marketing must take priority, I realized, because everything else flows from that.

Here's what we did:

- We invested a fortune in creating sales leads. I look at every lead, no matter how small, as gold. These potential clients have already decided they're going to spend money to celebrate. That business is there for the taking, and we must go for it.
- Each team member is held accountable for timely contact. We reassign leads when a salesperson is sluggish on response time.

People want to buy when they are ready to buy, not when we're ready to sell to them.
- We also communicate on our customers' timetable, not ours, with salespeople available some nights and weekends. We aim to achieve a first-mover sales closing advantage.
- We set goals for each team member, ensuring buy-in by working with them. Of course, the goals are higher for more senior team members.
- Team members who reach a certain sales goal earn the right to their own sales coordinator, who provides admin and sales support.
- Team members are expected to attend each one of the events they sell but are NOT responsible for the execution—they're there to communicate the clients' needs to my culinary, ops, and warehouse teams.
- Each week we track the number of leads, as well as those leads that are turned into opportunities (potential business). Then we track each client along the sales cycle, even projecting closing probabilities based on how far along our client mentoring has gone. (Notice I said "mentoring," not selling. Great salespeople mentor before they sell.)
- We keep all team members up to date with sales progress. Keeping your sales status secret rather than transparent will lead to unrest, as team members wonder if there will be future work for them.
- We require team members to participate in sales training online and ask them to share what they've learned along the way.
- For every closed contract, my sales director and I send out congratulations to the team member and companywide. We also provide bonuses and simple celebrations, with cake being everyone's favorite treat.

- We assign to each sales team member a list of contacts: venues where we can cater, bridal and corporate planners, and destination management companies that serve incentive and corporate groups traveling to South Florida. The team members are responsible for maintaining relationships with these contacts, and if they fail to do so, we'll reassign the contact to someone else. We require our sales team members to focus on these heavy hitters because they represent multiple weddings and events, rather than simply one company or one couple.

One of the best ways to focus your sales efforts on clients that represent multiple sales is by selling B2B—from one business to another, rather than from business to consumer.

Years ago, I played golf with an insurance agent who insured multiple cars sitting on dealer lots, rather than selling door to door, one car at a time. He knew how to use his sales-and-marketing time wisely—when he closed one dealer, with hundreds of cars on the lot, his insurance fees would be in the six figures. That's a much bigger paycheck than he'd get insuring one family car at a time.

In 2021 I purchased a firm called Different Look with another successful B2B model. This tabletop rental company only works with hotels, wedding planners, caterers, and country clubs. Monica Festinger, the company's original owner, made the decision with her former partner to focus on clients who represent multiple sales rather than a single sale. A bride, for example, would only need their products once. But venues and planners, who are in the wedding business, will place large orders again and again. The sales team can build much more fruitful relationships with these companies that will continue to pay off. (Because Monica and I owned Different Look and Alexander Catering as 50/50 partners, we decided in July 2023 that she keep Different Look and I take Alexander Catering, which has worked out well for both of us.)

Rewards along with consequences go a long way toward keeping a sales team on track and engaged. Like many companies, we discovered the benefits of working from home after the onset of the COVID pandemic. Our sales team members now enjoy that perk. Most weekday mornings, we meet on Zoom for up to half an hour. Our team members save commute time on days when they have no in-person meetings.

One challenge in dealing with commissioned sales team members is keeping everyone in their own lanes. Each producer has his or her own venues and clients, but assigning other leads needs to be fair and give us the best chance of closing.

Obviously, the top performers receive the better leads at times, and senior team members have developed relationships with the best clients over the years. Yet no one holds the juniors back from doing the same. Catering sales—and sales in general—are all about relationship-building.

And that includes relationship-building within your own team. My senior management team and I support the sales staff by giving them the tools and resources they need to succeed.

As the leader, each morning I take a long, hard look in the mirror and remind myself of these words by author John Maxwell: "A good leader is a person who takes a little more than his share of the blame and a little less than his share of the credit."

It should go without saying, but a sales team will refuse to be accountable if the sales manager consistently owns the successes but deflects the failures.

Ultimately, your team expects you to lead by example. That means defending the efforts of your team as well as celebrating their efforts publicly. For us, these strategies have paid off. Sales are soaring, and 2024 is on track to be our best year ever.

DEFINE YOUR BRAND—THEN SPREAD THE WORD!

Branding strategists can transform small companies into powerhouses—it's one of the best investments a business owner can make.

Last decade, I engaged a branding firm to help me define my brands. If you have the budget to hire one, you can skip to the next section. But if not, then let's dig deeper into the seven components of a brand statement.

A great brand statement should do the following:

- Define your business.
- Share your values.
- State your brand's promise.
- Differentiate you from your competition.
- Identify your market position.
- Clearly state your message.
- Let clients know what to expect from you.

Here's my catering firm's brand statement:

> *At Bill Hansen Catering, perfection is our goal. In our fifth decade in catering and event planning, Bill Hansen has the expertise to ensure your event is one to remember. Today, his full-service catering and event design company is known throughout South Florida for exceptional events, visionary design, and creative cuisine. Whether you have a sweet tooth or prefer adventurous dishes from across the world, we will cater to you. Bill Hansen custom menus are designed with you in mind—that's to say that no other event in the state will enjoy your exclusive menu. Thanks to our extensive knowledge of world cuisine, we'll develop a menu that reflects your tastes and leaves no detail unaccounted for. Regardless of your unique vision, count on Bill and his team to cater divine cuisine for any event under the Florida sun.*

When you read this description, you can clearly see that our Bill Hansen brand is upscale; we are not the low-price choice. We are all about delighting our clients and their guests with unique and innovative experiences, and we do more than just cater—we can create the complete experience for our clients. We're more than just a food service.

During my time in business, marketing has advanced from ads in the Yellow Pages to fax machines to websites to social media, including TikTok, and AI.

I built my first website in 1995, when my son Jimmy suggested I investigate the internet. I replied, "The what-a-net?"

"Dad," he said, "you need to get with the times." And I did, with the help of some younger technical minds.

I've lost count of the number of websites I've built, and the number of website "gurus" that I've hired and fired. I've finally found a firm that builds all my sites at a fraction of the cost of other designers: LocaliQ. I swear by these folks. Not only do they build websites, they handle such marketing needs as display ads, YouTube ads, search engine optimization, and more. Log onto these sites to see the results:

www.hansengroup.co
www.billhansencatering.com
www.villa-woodbine.com
www.lovablescatering.com
www.billhansenmiamivenues.com

I've tried outsourcing my social media and found this to be a huge mistake. Your social media folks should be employees or an independent contractor that works primarily on your account, rather than someone from a social media firm who is handling many accounts. They should live and breathe all that goes into your company's brand and story.

Currently, my marketing team includes two talented members. We meet weekly to discuss strategy, tasks, and results. We examine not only the number of visitors to our sites, but engagement time "stickiness." Each week, we review the following:

- Number of Instagram and Facebook followers added
- Number of hours users spend on our websites

- Number of new venues added to the Bill Hansen Miami Venues site
- Number of leads generated

I'm a huge fan of LinkedIn, with more than 21,000 connections. The super-achiever in me is shooting for 30,000 connections—the max allowed.

LinkedIn helps me qualify clients. Couples I can find on LinkedIn are generally likely to be able to afford my services. Planners I find on LinkedIn are of a higher caliber and more likely to work with us. Corporate clients I find on LinkedIn are usually higher up the chain of command and are more likely to be the decision-makers, not the gatekeepers.

Expand your LinkedIn connections by connecting with everyone who crosses your path. It's not only who you know, but who knows you … and LinkedIn expands your marketing borders exponentially.

However, don't rely solely on virtual networking! A warm smile, a firm grip, and even a big hug go a long way toward cementing business friendships. A decade ago, I started a group called Focus Miami, with the intent of generating summertime wedding and event business—our slow season in South Florida. Summers are still slow here—we can't change the weather—but we created a strong networking alliance of planners, caterers, and vendors. We meet monthly at different venues, and leads are passed along at every meeting.

If you're an extrovert like me, you are perfect for networking. If you're an introvert, bring along an extrovert for your networking activities.

Chambers of Commerce and business groups such as BNI (Business Network International) can be invaluable for expanding your circles. BNI generates the most leads for the least amount of financial investment. But keep in mind—if you join these groups, you need to attend the meetings, schedule one-on-ones with other members, refer leads to other members, and attend the social events.

You can't be a passive member and expect any results. Although the dollar investment is small, you will need to plan on investing a few hours a week to be successful. As a member of the Miami Beach Chamber of Commerce for five years, I continue to cherish the friends I made and the referrals that continue to bring me business.

Another marketing option is to partner with nonprofits, offering a reduced price in exchange for media exposure. My company gets bombarded with requests from nonprofits, and I like to give where I get. "Who in your organization has hired my firm before?" I'll ask. Another key question: "What media and promotional exposure will my firm receive in exchange for our donation?"

Don't get me wrong, "generosity" is my middle name, and I don't always give to get. My lifetime goal is to become a "reverse-tither," giving away 90 percent of what I earn to worthy causes. But I do this with my personal funds. When it comes to my businesses, I need to determine my ROI before sharing time, talent, and treasure with worthy organizations.

How much should you invest in marketing? And how do you know what's working and what's not? For one thing, as Henry Ford said, "Stopping advertising to save money is like stopping your watch to save time."

I've learned that print ads don't work for me, so I stay away from those slick luxury magazines who wish to barter advertising for catering. Big mistake.

And don't forget—sales and marketing are two different animals. Marketing generates leads, and the sales team closes them.

For reference, the U.S. Small Business Administration recommends spending 7 to 8 percent of your gross revenue on marketing and advertising if you're doing less than $5 million a year in sales and your net profit margin—after all expenses—is in the 10 to 12 percent range.

Remember: You get 80 percent of your leads from 20 percent of your marketing. Focus on the 20 percent that brings you the 80 percent, not the 80 percent that brings you the 20 percent. The only way to determine this is to track where your leads originate. Focus your efforts on what gets the most bang for your marketing buck.

NURTURE RELATIONSHIPS

> *"Always remember that everyone with whom you have a relationship has an invisible sign on their forehead that says, 'Make Me Feel Important.' Treat them accordingly."*
>
> —**Eric Philip Cowell**, property developer, music industry executive, and father of Simon Cowell

Exceptional sales and marketing is relationship-based, not price-based. It focuses on first selling the company and its people, then on selling the products, and finally on the price. I've learned there are myriad ways to nurture relationships while expanding your borders. In fact, you can make it a goal to develop new and deeper relationships daily.

"Always be closing!" Remember that line uttered by the abusive sales trainer played by Alec Baldwin in *Glengarry Glen Ross*? Well, my friend Chris Sanchez, managing partner of LUX Catering & Events in Salt Lake City—who's as upbeat and friendly as the Baldwin character is negative and threatening—has a corollary: "Always be ready."

One day, Chris had less than 45 minutes to prepare for a big client who had been referred by the venue the client had just selected—and he was not looking forward to it. "I was thinking, 'Nobody's here. The building's a mess. We just finished a big event,'" recalls Chris. "I was panicked."

The client walked in and fired off a list of requirements for the event—including just a one-month lead time. She slapped down a credit card, basically giving Chris and his team an unlimited budget to work with. "It ended up being our largest event to date," says

Chris of the $2,500-per-head gala that included heads of state and military generals. "It was magnificent."

For Chris, the event was a lesson in preparedness. "You never know what's going to happen," he notes. "How many times have I or any of us been at an event, and suddenly, up walks your next big client? You're tired, you've been running around, and they're ready to talk to you about an event."

You have to be "on," stresses Chris, even if you feel "off." One way to do that is to tap into the excitement you feel for your profession. Remember why you do what you do—and model that enthusiasm for your staff as well.

Anyone in the service industry is in the people business. Therefore, connecting with customers and prospects is your primary job. How can you start making those connections? By listening! As the Greek philosopher Epictetus said, "We have two ears and one mouth so that we can listen twice as much as we speak."

Ask questions—and then really listen to the answers.

Research potential customers online before meeting them, and jot down a few questions to ask to get the conversation started. Your goal is to find something you have in common with them.

Granted, a senior citizen like me who's been around the block a few times can usually find something in common with only a few questions, such as "Where are you from?" One of my salespeople lived all over the country, so more times than not, she could find something to relate to. (And, not that I recommend this, but there were times when she stretched the truth a little.)

As you proceed past the pleasantries, it's useful for salespeople to arm themselves with questions to learn more about what customers want. Inspired by the book *Power Questions* by Andrew Sobel and Jerold Panas, my team asks questions like these to maximize their sales success:

- What would be useful for you to know about our firm?
- What prompted your interest in our meeting?

- Given what we've set out in our proposal, and thinking about value to you, can you say something about what you'd like to see more or less of?
- What do you like most about the approach we've outlined?
- What aspects concern you?
- In thinking about choosing a partner to work with on this, what's most important to you?
- May I ask who else are you talking to?
- Who will make the final decision about choosing a firm to work with?
- If two providers are evenly matched in terms of technical ability, experience, and price, how will you make the decision?
- I sense you have some hesitation. Can you help me understand what is behind that?
- Is there anyone else who we ought to discuss this with or hear from before we finalize our approach?

I've built my business by encouraging my teams to act as consultants—not as salespeople. There is a huge difference. Consultants ask the right questions at the right time and listen carefully to the answers. Salespeople, on the other hand, often talk too much and listen even less. They can be pushy, forgetting about the "two ears and one mouth" rule. Many ask for the sale before it's the right time. Consultants, too, ask for the sale, but they wait for cues from the client.

Decades ago, my partner Bill and I were asked to cater for the first Miami Grand Prix in downtown Miami. To learn more, we traveled to the left coast of the U.S. to observe catering at the Long Beach Grand Prix. We studied ways we could cater for these large crowds of race fans and came up with ways to do it better. Rather than leaving food sitting on warming devices for hours, for example, we planned to serve *à la minute*, cooking for customers as needed. However, we forgot that the Miami Grand Prix was held on the same weekend that we were catering another mega event, and we didn't have the bandwidth to do both. (We did have a fun weekend in La-La Land, though.)

Even though the business didn't pan out, we showed our potential client that we were willing to go the extra mile (or, in that case, many extra miles). My team and I build relationships with our clients by doing more than expected. That includes creating a custom menu rather than insisting clients conform to boilerplate menus. Other ways great businesses go the extra mile include taking the time to check with competitors when they're out of an item a customer wants, and special ordering an item for a good customer.

Recently, one of my front teeth fell out on a holiday weekend, and my dentist came in on a Sunday to keep my smile so wide I could eat a banana sideways. Then he personally followed up to make sure I was feeling OK. Like my dentist, my team works to connect and engage with customers, which results in deeper relationships—and, of course, more revenue.

Another way to deepen relationships with clients is to deliver products and services on time or early. In the sales process, quick response times are crucial. We train our staff to answer the phone in less than three rings and to return calls immediately—never more than 24 hours later. Most basic proposals can be created in a day or two. People want things "rapido," as we say in Miami. And being the first mover in client relations is a surefire way to build upon relationships while your competition lags way behind in response times.

NEVER STOP SALES TRAINING

The COVID-19 pandemic ushered in dark days for everyone—and the catering industry was especially hard hit. In March 2020 we watched our full calendar of business dwindle to nothing as clients canceled events left and right. After the lockdown, caterers across the country struggled to keep the doors open. Many couldn't.

While the future was uncertain, I decided to double-down on my business. We kept on our entire sales team and invested in a sales training program created by Grant Cardone, whose own team we had catered an event for. The program inspired us all—and we were ready to implement its strategies as soon as we could start booking events again.

Training and communicating with your sales team should never stop. In our meetings, we iron out issues and conduct sales training lessons, which results in very low sales team turnover and good spirits.

Don't make the mistake of keeping your sales team siloed. After all, salespeople must know what they're selling. Our sales team reviews forthcoming events with operations and culinary weekly, and at least once a month we meet in person to share new policies with the complete team, as well as discuss ways we can improve. The weekly meeting is about working *in* the business, and the monthly meeting is working *on* the business to improve how we operate.

Like anyone in sales, I've experienced highs and lows in my career—from landing a job to cater for President and Mrs. Reagan and Pope John Paul II in 1987 to losing out on a big catered event for Coca-Cola a couple of years later (one of my former employees reeled that one in).

No one ever trained me in how to deal with these setbacks. Yet I believe that owners, managers, and sales leaders should not only celebrate successes but also help and nurture team members when they suffer a sales defeat.

I used to keep a file full of lost proposals labeled "Learning Experiences." After each failed sale, I'd set out to learn why I came up short. Some questions I'd ask myself—and that I encourage sales team members to ask themselves—are:

- Did I talk too much instead of listen?
- Did I sell the experience and the value, or focus too much on the price?
- Did I focus on features rather than benefits? For example, a ballpoint pen may have a clip on it as well as a retractable tip. Those are features. The benefits are the pen staying in a pocket

(because of the clip) without ink soiling the user's clothes (because of the retractable tip). Great food and service are features; the benefits are guests being happy and the client looking good.
- Did I ask for the sale, or simply skirt around it?
- Did I adequately respond to objections?
- Was I selling to the wrong person and not the decision-maker?
- Did I do my homework prior to the meeting?

As a business owner, manager, or supervisor, you can bolster your team members' spirits with a pep talk. And to get them back on track, send them another lead immediately that has a high probability of closing quickly. There's nothing like a close to boost confidence, which will lead to more sales.

GET THE MOST BANG FOR YOUR DAILY BUCK OF TIME

Dialing for Dollars. That's what my former colleague used to call sales prospecting.

You've probably been on the other end of these calls, either at work or at home. It doesn't get more annoying than when the phone trills in the middle of a family dinner and a telemarketer is on the line.

But, if you think about it, if those calls didn't work, why would they keep calling?

The same goes for sales prospecting (though I'd never advise my team to call someone's home number or try to reach a prospect after normal business hours).

In a company like mine, our team needs to prospect to generate revenue.

Yes, people can find us; we're all over the internet and social media, but our competition is out there, too. So, when a person needs catering, given a handful of good choices, who will they call? Usually, it's the person who has been in touch on a regular basis, who has built a relationship. Many times, it's the person who has "touched" them last.

So how do you find sales prospects? I know it's old-fashioned, but exchanging business cards is a great start. Personally, I burn through 50 or more a week. I'm always handing them out, and I ask for one in return.

You can purchase prospecting lists. Or you can find prospects by scouring social media. For example, I find bridal planners on LinkedIn and reach out to them. I also like to qualify a potential customer on social media to see if he or she is in our target market. For example, as I was editing this manuscript, I received a lead for a wedding at the Bonnet House in Fort Lauderdale. I quickly found out the potential client is an attorney in Delray Beach, which gives us some background before we contact her. I also sent her an invitation to connect on LinkedIn.

Past clients are excellent prospects. Whatever business you're in, these clients are low-hanging fruit. In my business, we may cater a customer's engagement party, rehearsal dinner, wedding, farewell brunch, baby shower, birthday parties, wedding anniversaries, and even the weddings for the customer's children. They're true clients for life—the best clients to have.

If you lost business to a competitor, follow up with that one-time prospect. Perhaps your competitor "blinked" and didn't live up to expectations—leaving the door open for you.

Once you've received a response from a prospect, the next step is to build that relationship.

You do this by showing that you care, and by quickly responding to each request. In the catering industry, you'd be surprised how many caterers simply don't get back to clients. (Some do it for a reason—to play hard to get, making it seem like the customer needs them more than they need the customer.)

Depending upon the size of the business opportunity, perks might help get a fish on the line—lunch, dinner, gifts, and tickets to sporting events and concerts can help reel those prospects in.

Sales is not for the faint of heart, and persistence pays. Occasionally, we have what we call "a hole in one," where a client books my venue Villa Woodbine sight unseen or on the first tour—but it's usually not that easy.

Depending on the type of business, it can take as many as 20 touchpoints to close a deal. Clients may "ghost" you, disappearing into cyberspace, but a great salesperson will persist until they get a "yes" or a firm "no."

I tell my sales team to put themselves in the shoes of a car buyer. You go into the showroom, love the vehicle, and then go home to talk about it. And then things may happen—an illness, a financial issue, a work problem that eats up your time. You still would like to buy that car, but it's not your immediate focus. If the salesperson continues to follow up, eventually it will be the right time.

We all hate those incessant calls, text messages, and emails, yet creative salespeople don't spam. They inform, and they offer suggestions and tips to their prospects.

For example, if our salesperson has been talking to a couple about their upcoming wedding but they haven't committed to us yet, we may entice them with a special offer—such as a complimentary welcome drink for their guests. Another enticement that works is a complimentary upgrade to their menu (and then negotiating a special price from your vendor). Or perhaps negotiate a special price with one of your other vendors and pass along that cost savings. All of these are reasons to contact a potential customer and hopefully close the deal.

One final suggestion for staying in touch—pass along the latest news about your firm or share a hot industry trend. Whatever keeps the lines of communication open eases the way to sales success.

Here's a tip: Allocate time daily for prospecting. Great salespeople know this, blocking out an hour or two each day to communicate with potential clients—not by making annoying calls to people at their homes, but by reaching out to offer information and simply checking in to see how a prospect is doing.

Prospecting for some is a grueling task. But it's part of the job. The problem arises when salespeople fail to block out time, first thing in the morning, to do their prospecting.

Instead, they can't wait to read their email. And those emails are time-sucks. Worse, they usually involve someone else demanding their time. Some people refer to time as "whirlwind" and "non-whirlwind" time. Whirlwind time is frequently wasted answering emails, returning phone calls, and even doing what your boss wants you to do—things that are urgent but often not important.

Non-whirlwind time is the time you make to do those things that are not necessarily urgent but extremely important.

And that's what prospecting is. It's not necessarily pleasant when people don't return your calls, answer your emails, or like you on social media. But time spent doing this will pay dividends beyond measure in the future. And since it's hard work, just like working out, it's best to do it first thing in the morning and get it out of the way.

TEAMWORK MAKES THE SALES DREAM WORK

My Navy boss, Captain Kash, called the Navy club system in the 1960s and 1970s "a group of independent dukedoms in a loosely federated state." In other words, each club was doing its own thing, even though we were all under the same umbrella.

Don't let your company devolve into a kingdom of independent dukedoms. It's an easy trap to fall into—different departments try to protect their own turf, creating a silo effect in which no one knows what anyone else is doing. This disfunction becomes especially disastrous when the sales team sells a product or service without the buy-in of those who must deliver it.

During the pandemic, our motto was "cash is king," and we would sell catering with little regard for the actual cost just to generate much-needed cash. We were struggling to stay solvent.

While that mindset helped us survive, it's not sustainable and can lead to problems. For example, during our "cash is king" phase, we sold an event some 50 miles from our commissary at a low price without checking the logistics of the venue. Turns out, there was no parking for the staff, so we needed to shuttle workers from a municipal parking lot over a mile away, requiring extra parking charges and one extra vehicle. We had to eat those costs since sales and operations hadn't communicated properly. If they had, we could have added the charges to the client's proposal.

Another example from the catering world is a salesperson who sells a menu with a food item that's not in season or is hard to find. That causes extra work for the culinary team and can adversely impact the event's gross margin.

Communication should flow both ways. For example, the warehouse and culinary teams should let the sales team know when there's extra inventory of an item to sell or when we're getting a great price on a certain product. The sales team can then push those items, leading to greater profit margins.

As wonderful as Zoom, Skype, and Google Meet are, in-person meetings remain critical. At our mandatory in-person monthly meetings for the sales, operations, and culinary teams, management shares ideas for improvement, while each attendee is asked to come up with an idea that will benefit the company as a whole. Sometimes there's a strict agenda, and other times we just talk and get to know each other better. Even the team's introverts speak up—which is harder to do on Zoom when people sometimes talk over each other and it's hard to read facial expressions.

We've also learned to involve all three departments in the proposal preparation to ensure that pricing is correct from the get-go, that the menu is perfect, and that our team can logistically perform the event, wherever it is. In our business, we may be catering an event on an island in the Everglades, in a high-rise apartment or commercial skyscraper, or at a historical site with strict rules and regulations. Our territory ranges from Palm Beach to the Florida Keys. With so many variables, ironing out logistics with all relevant departments is crucial.

VERTICALLY INTEGRATE

When I ask my catering management students at Florida International University what catering means to them, they usually reply something along the lines of: "It's food dropped off on platters and in chafing dishes." And for some firms, that's true. One catering company in my market has a fleet of vans doing these drop-offs seven days a week. They're coining money.

My business, however, is mainly full-service catering—we provide the food, the staff, the tables, chairs, linens, chinaware, flatware, and stemware, along with the bar and beverages.

But my ambitions go beyond that. We want to be the go-to ultimate resource for all clients who are planning weddings, parties, corporate events, mitzvahs, quinceañeras, and celebrations of every kind.

We are becoming a one-stop shop for everything our clients may need, including event planning, design, décor, room blocks for destination weddings, ground transportation, photography, videography, and venue sourcing. We also can provide specialty catering options, including glatt kosher and Indian (which we outsource), and other menu choices created in-house by my corporate executive chef, Dewey LoSasso.

Obviously, the more of these "extras" we add to our invoice, the more revenue we generate.

In short, we are focused on vertically integrating—either owning aspects of the business that previously would be farmed out to external contractors or suppliers, or establishing relationships with approved vendors who allow us to sell their services at a discount.

One of the challenges in selling these upgrades is that clients can go direct. If a client goes direct to one of our vendors, they will pay retail and must handle all the logistics on their own. We make sure clients know the time and hassle they're saving by booking these services with us. We charge a management fee of 22.5 percent and take on the responsibility for delivery, set-up, and breakdown. Most clients love the convenience and happily pay for it.

Here's another example that's right in my backyard. The famous Joe's Stone Crab in Miami Beach doesn't buy stone crabs from just anyone—in fact, the restaurant doesn't buy them at all. They employ their own fleet of fishing boats to catch the stone crabs that have garnered fans worldwide.

Similarly, more and more catering companies are vertically integrating the food that they serve. One Miami caterer owns a hydroponic garden in the city's Overtown neighborhood, supplying him with local, farm-fresh produce that he can incorporate into his menus.

When you capture more of the supply chain for your business, you're gaining control of elements your customers are buying anyway. That leads to higher sales—and higher profits.

CHAPTER 5
TEAMWORK
CULTURE EATS STRATEGY FOR BREAKFAST

MANAGEMENT GURU PETER DRUCKER FAMOUSLY said, "Culture eats strategy for breakfast." In other words, company culture determines business success—regardless of those pie-in-the-sky "Strategic Plans."

It's proven true for me. As much as I try to be a strategic thinker, I've discovered what's even more important: surrounding myself with people smarter than me, giving them the tools to do their jobs, and creating a workplace culture that fulfills our core values.

No matter how detailed and solid your strategy is, if the people executing it don't model the appropriate culture, your projects will fail.

And culture isn't about comfy chairs, breakroom ping-pong tables, or happy hours at the office. Rather, it's about the ways your employees act in critical situations, how they manage pressure and respond to various challenges, and how they treat partners, customers, and each other.

As the leader of my tribe of service, sales, and culinary professionals, it's my job to model these behaviors daily. In the wise words of Confucian scholar Xunzi: "What I hear, I forget. What I see, I remember. What I do, I understand."

This chapter breaks down the top eight cultural behaviors for business success. They should inspire you to take a fresh look at your own culture and make changes where you're falling short.

GIVE EMPLOYEES WHAT THEY NEED

Motivational speaker Simon Sinek recounts a time he asked a barista whether he liked his job. Without batting an eye, the guy said that he loved *this* job. On the other hand, the barista continued, he counted the hours until quitting time at another hotel where he also served up lattes.

The barista performed the same job at two different companies. How could he love one but hate the other? Turns out, it all boiled down to *culture*. At the first place, the barista's bosses asked how he was doing and what he needed. At the second? They watched to see when he would screw up.

Sometimes, with all the talk about the entrepreneur's lifestyle and freedom, we forget that entrepreneurship isn't simply about "leading" or "being in charge." It's also about serving and providing what people need—especially the very employees that some look down upon. They're the real reasons why we exist. Particularly in service jobs, team members may be treated poorly by customers. It's our job to lift them up and give them the motivation to perform to the best of their abilities.

Remember, team members can't perform well without the proper training—regardless of their experience. Whenever I dine out, I watch the servers to observe whether they serve food from the left, the right, or at random. We serve food from the left, with the left hand, and with the left foot forward. This is covered in our basic server training program when team members are hired, and we provide refresher training prior to shifts. But without training, how would a server know that this is the best way to avoid getting in the way of a guest's arm?

At Houston's A Fare Extraordinaire, all chairs must be covered after every event—and therefore the chairs last longer and look better than they would otherwise. Upon hearing about this task, someone said to owner Rachael Volz, "Oh my gosh, I bet your staff hates you for that!"

The opposite is true, as Rachael explained to the tactless commenter: Employees appreciate knowing exactly how to do their jobs. Rachael has meticulous standards that she imparts to team members—if there's a weed in the parking lot, pull it; if there's a sticker on an avocado, peel it off before it goes into the compost heap. This attention to detail has led to the company's success in a very competitive market.

"I'm very, very clear on my expectations," says Rachael. "And really smart, ambitious people love to work in an environment like that, because you weed out all of the bad apples."

If you're the leader of the company, your attitude sets the tone for the rest of the team. "One can't underestimate the importance of walking into the office as the boss with a smile on my face and making sure I give the same feeling of importance to everyone," said Jon Sumroy, CEO and founder of Mifold, which originated the foldable grab-and-go booster seat.

I couldn't agree more. Team members also need prayers. Yes, controversial, but regardless of their beliefs in a higher power, prayers matter. I regularly pray one-on-one with team members who come and ask me to pray with them for their health and the health of their family members, for their financial challenges, or simply for encouragement.

An experience I had one day with one of my female cooks warmed my heart. I found her sobbing outside my Broward commissary. I jumped out of my SUV and rushed to her side, prepared for the worst. I assumed something had happened in the kitchen that forced her to go outside and cool off, or that my executive chef had terminated her.

Turns out, her husband's business was growing, and he needed her to work there full-time rather than part-time. She was crying tears of regret since she loved working for us, and this was her final exit from a workplace she cherished.

Although I was sad to see her leave, it gave me joy to know we had created a workplace that people loved and valued.

SHOW MEANINGFUL APPRECIATION

In the rough-and-tumble world of foodservice, it's not easy for a business to keep its doors open for decades. And only a select few can boast that they've been serving customers for over a century.

So Morin's in Attleboro, Massachusetts, established in 1911, must be doing something right. The founder's grandson—my Cornell classmate Russ Morin—is president of the company's catering division, Russell Morin Catering & Events. Russ made the decision early in his tenure to take care of his team members.

In 1976, Russ implemented a profit-sharing plan, paid time off, and medical benefits—long before they were common. Employee perks have grown since then, with the multimillion-dollar company offering such incentives as tuition reimbursement.

Russ understands that his company will only survive another hundred years with committed, long-term team members—and he makes sure they know they're valued.

One of my mantras is: Nobody cares how much you know, until they know how much you care. I care deeply about team members such as Thelma Corea, who has worked with me for five decades.

She's one of a group of women who helped my company succeed in its early years. Many of these employees are immigrants from Nicaragua. They don't hold degrees from culinary schools, and a few don't even have high school diplomas. But they stand proud on their feet all day in our cold food kitchen, crafting the best handmade hors d'oeuvres in Miami.

These ladies left their war-torn country for the U.S. with nothing but their clothes, and many now own their own homes as they watch their offspring succeed. Working alongside 15-year veteran Patty Ordenada, for example, are her daughter and mother, while her son serves in the U.S. Marine Corps. Thelma and her son own lakefront homes in North Miami.

I recall one day trying to make spinach and feta in phyllo pastry by myself in the kitchen (we make our own rather than buy ready-made). I struggled with this simple task, each pastry looking worse than the last. The goal was to create equilateral triangles, but my attempts resulted in all sorts of geometric shapes too ugly to serve.

The Nicaraguan kitchen squad saw my feeble attempts, shooed me out of the way, grabbed the flimsy pastry strips, and created perfectly formed mini bites in no time.

These ladies are like family to Terry and me, and we wanted to show them how much they meant to us. But how could we show our appreciation in a meaningful way? We decided to take them on an all-expenses-paid trip back to Nicaragua.

We flew into Managua and visited their schools and their former homes, some with dirt floors. The first night we stayed in an island home on Lake Nicaragua, sipping Flor de Caña rum while lying in hammocks. The next morning, a local woman arrived via rowboat, armed with freshly laid eggs for breakfast.

Then we were off to the mountainous coffee country, where we dined on the best grass-fed steak I've ever had. Finally, we ventured to the coastal town of Corinto, Thelma's hometown, where we stuffed ourselves with platters of freshly caught seafood. It was a journey none of us will ever forget.

While we haven't taken all our employees on memorable trips, we make sure they know they're appreciated. I handwrite notes for our full-timers' birthdays, for example, and sometimes we celebrate more extravagantly.

In 1995, one of my team members, Michael Meltzer (who now owns his own catering firm), worked on his birthday at a United Way fundraiser at a mansion on Star Island. The multi-million-dollar estate happened to be the home of Gloria and Emilio Estefan.

The Estefans are the real deal, even instructing their staff to serve us freshly squeezed lemonade as we set up the event in the sweltering summertime heat and humidity.

We brought a cake along as a surprise for Michael after the party, and the Estefans let us linger awhile as we celebrated in style.

Recently, I traveled to Las Vegas to speak at a conference (I go to Lost Wages once a year to visit my money). While there, one of my team members back home won a cultural behavior badge. I sent a video of myself congratulating her. It's a small thing, but it meant a lot to her, and she knows I appreciate all she does for my company.

Showing meaningful appreciation is one of my cultural pillars that has helped me build a company where people feel appreciated for who they are, not simply for what they do.

FOCUS ON CULTURE BEFORE HIRING

A successful company culture often hinges on who you let in the door. Let's face it—some people have innate personality traits that prevent them from being team players. Instead of fighting a losing battle and trying to change those employees, create hiring practices to ensure you're selecting candidates with the right attitude and instincts.

My first sales hire was an empty-nester housewife, Janet McDonald, who agreed to work for commission only. Even though Janet didn't have any sales experience, I saw traits in her that I knew would be invaluable—she dressed and carried herself well, was well connected in Miami social circles, and had the gift of gab while knowing how to listen. Perhaps most importantly, Janet was persistent. She didn't quit until she got a "yes" or a "no," and sometimes she skillfully turned a "no" into a "yes." Janet called her sales follow-up routine "checking her traps."

She ended up being a natural, growing her business from $250,000 in the first year to $1 million in her fourth year.

While that was a hiring success story, finding new salespeople and team members in general is not easy, particularly in today's economy.

Executive recruiter David Kohlasch of Patrice & Associates looks for two personality traits when interviewing candidates for sales director positions: leadership skills and emotional intelligence.

"One sign of a great leader is the number of people he or she has developed," says David. To help determine if a candidate has been a nurturing mentor, he'll ask a question such as: "Could you tell me about some of the people you've taken under your wing and how they grew as a result of your tutelage?" If the candidate speaks warmly and excitedly about former mentees, chances are he or she will be committed to the success of the entire team.

Emotional intelligence can be gauged by asking situational questions about how the candidate reacted when tensions were about to explode. Here are two examples David uses:

1. "How would you handle a team member who raged into your office demanding immediate answers?"

2. "How did you react when you learned that a major client was very unhappy and disturbed about his latest order?"

Answers to questions such as these can help determine how professional a candidate will be, and how well he or she will get along with the rest of the team.

Of course, hiring mistakes happen even with a well-thought-out vetting system. In that case, don't be like the sports team owner who doesn't want to admit that he made a mistake with his top draft pick, keeping his dud player on for far too long. As I like to say, "If you have to swallow a frog, you don't want to look at it very long." Cut your losses—as soon as you realize you need to.

Here's another strategy for getting to know potential employees before hiring them: Teach a class in your field. Since 1990 I've taught a catering management course at Florida International University (FIU). There, I've been able to find the best and the brightest, bringing them on as servers, then sales coordinators, and finally salespeople.

At FIU, not only do I see how potential employees behave as students, I see them in action. For each class, my students and I produce an event. In 2021, for example, we produced a complimentary wedding for a deserving couple. We've also put on fundraisers, raising close to half a million dollars for worthy causes. After observing various students in these high-pressure situations, I've hired many of them as both full- and part-time team members. They've all lived up to their promise, with many proving to be rising stars.

If you don't have the time to teach a course, volunteer as a guest lecturer in a college course related to your industry. Instructors like me welcome breaks, and the students love to hear from industry experts. Encourage students to reach out to you after the class. The ambitious ones will—and you may find your next rock-star employee from that lecture class.

DETERMINE WHAT YOUR CULTURE IS

"Go find Joe, and he'll show you what to do." I'd bet every caterer has used similar words on a Saturday night in December.

With the peaks and valleys of our seasonal work, sometimes catering newbies must hit the ground running and not stop until the guests have left and the trucks are loaded. We're not like Disney or other big corporations, where new hires do months of training and indoctrination.

Even if a new employee gets thrown into the fray, he or she must attend in-person training. In training, we cover everything from attire, grooming, and behavior to basic service procedures. Most importantly, however, we ensure new team members understand the company culture.

At Bill Hansen Catering, our culture is built on love and kindness. We encourage team members to:

- Love what you do—and show it.
- Love serving others—and show it.
- Be kind to fellow team members.

No yelling or screaming is allowed. We aim to stay calm, cool, and collected when dealing with the inevitable crises that arise during an event. Remedial action is done in private with care, not in public (unless necessary to avoid an accident).

Many commercial kitchens are hotbeds of dissent. Cooks yell and scream at one another. Ours, however, is a well-oiled machine, with little chit-chat and a strong focus on quality and teamwork.

Since empathy is at the root of treating others well, our training involves familiarizing team members with all aspects of the business. For example, sales coordinators don't just learn how to be sales coordinators. Part of their training involves spending time in the culinary and operations departments, and with me. This way, they get a better overview of the entire company and gain an understanding of how their work can be helped or hindered by their relationships with peers in other departments.

I've learned that the larger an organization grows, the more important communication becomes. I'd say 80 percent of problems in any business are due to inefficient and ineffective communication. And things grow worse as silos begin to rise in the departments—staff members start thinking they need to protect their turf instead of acting collaboratively. One of my jobs is ensuring that these silos don't grow—or, better yet, never get off the ground to begin with.

Building team culture isn't for the faint-hearted. It's something I struggled with for years and years. Yes, my companies are good places to work, but I continue to try to make them great places to work. "People Before Profits" is my mantra. Because with great team members and culture, the profits will follow, and not at the expense of your team. We'll turn down profitable weddings and events if we see that potential clients aren't treating our team members respectfully and kindly.

Chris Villard, general manager of a catering company in Atlanta, puts it like this: "Our team are our clients as well. They can choose to work with us or not. And if we're not going to respect them and make sure that they are treated with value, they're not going to want to work for us. And I never want to put my team in that position."

Chris has fired wedding planners who treated staff members poorly. His company recently let go a client who brought in $500,000 a year because their corporate chef yelled at Chris's staff members, changed plans at the last minute, and didn't listen to the catering team's concerns and advice, resulting in chaotic situations and high stress for everyone.

"We told the client, 'You bring a lot of money to the table, but it's really not worth the headache and effort that we had to put in,'" says Chris. "If you don't have the same values we do, then we can't work together."

Recently, we've incorporated CultureWise in our HR program, which I learned about from my business coach in Vistage. CultureWise is a turnkey operating system for culture. Created by David J. Friedman, it's based on the leadership lessons he learned and taught in his decades as an award-winning CEO, speaker, author, and consultant. The CultureWise system has been implemented in more than 500 organizations in North America, helping them to better leverage their culture as a strategic competitive advantage.

Customers love doing business with companies that have great culture because a great culture resonates from the minds of the team members to the minds of their clients. And don't think you can't have a great culture because "it's always been like this." When Andy Levin became president of MHS Lift in Philadelphia, he inherited a "silo" culture where the sales, operations, and finance departments were operating independently. He reached the point of not wanting to go to work in the morning because of the sky-high tension between departments. Once the forklift firm implemented the CultureWise program with its 26 acceptable behaviors, however, everything turned around. For three straight years, starting in 2020, MHS Lift was named one of the top workplaces in the greater Philadelphia area by *The Philadelphia Inquirer*.

ADD FUN TO THE MIX

When Anthony Lambatos was in high school, he had an epiphany: Fun and productivity can go hand in hand.

Growing up, he worked at the catering business owned by his father—a taskmaster nicknamed "The Tornado," who had a reputation for yelling at his employees. While the company was successful, "turnover was high," says Anthony. "How people treated each other wasn't very good."

Anthony discovered a different way of doing things when his dad entrusted him with a 30-day concession contract while he was still in high school. Anthony hired his friends, they all wore Hawaiian shirts, and they played silly games while working, like keeping a tally of each customer sporting a mullet. Not only did the ad hoc team successfully and efficiently provide concessions, they had a blast while doing it.

"It shaped my whole idea of what it means to have fun at work," says Anthony. "When people understand their role, and they do it with people they love and respect, there's a magic that takes place."

When Anthony and his wife, April, bought out his father's business—Footers Catering in Denver—they set out to create an environment where people loved coming to work. One way they accomplished this is by forming a "culture club," made up of six team members representing every department in the company, with three members from the executive team. "A lot of people say, 'We have a culture club,' and it's someone from the front desk, the CEO's admin, and a bookkeeper, and they plan the Christmas party and the company picnic," notes Anthony. "That's not a culture club; that's a party-planning committee."

Footers' culture club promotes four initiatives with its activities:

1. Recognition
2. Relationships
3. Fun
4. Purpose

Every day at Footers, all employees eat together, family-style, with each department responsible for a task, such as making the food (the culinary team takes this one on, naturally), setting up, and cleaning up. Once a month during the "Lunch and Learn," an employee presents his or her origin story, complete with a slideshow. On Board Game Fridays, everyone chooses where to sit based on which game is on the table. "It's a good way to mix up who sits with whom," says Anthony.

Anthony also came up with a clever acronym for Footers' core values: FAB TIGERS, for Fun, Awesomeness, Balance, Teamwork, Innovation, Growth, Ethics, Respect, and Service. Employees earn Jimmy Bucks—named for Anthony's father—for demonstrating a core value, which they can spend in the company's swag store for hats, jackets, extra uniforms, and the like.

And there's more. Footers hosts four company-wide events each year—from a summer Olympics to a lip-sync battle—designed to engage everyone, even the part-timers. Employees earn paid-for vacations for every five years they are at the company. Footers even organizes optional company vacations, paying for a percentage of each attendee's costs.

Not only has Footers' collegial culture resulted in sky-high retention levels, but Anthony trains other hospitality companies—including Bill Hansen Catering—on how to make their workplaces fun and engaging. The training is named for one of Footers' missions: Make It Better Everyday, or MIBE.

To MIBE, explains Anthony, you have to be committed—all the time. "Culture isn't something you can just work on in the slow season," he stresses. "If you're going to commit to it, it has to be a part of every week. We're constantly making time for culture, no matter how busy we are."

ENCOURAGE TEAM MEMBERS TO SPEAK STRAIGHT

Your hiring decisions are the most important decisions you will ever make. I paid the price dearly when I made a bad hire for director of sales. He caused dissension among vendors and some clients—which I learned by listening to my team.

It's important to have an open door with your staff members, and to discern which concerns are real and which are self-serving. These were real, and sales sputtered under his leadership. Although I probably waited too long to terminate this person, he's gone, and I learned from my big mistake.

What you want to avoid are elephants in the room. Team members should feel they can speak freely without repercussion. At our weekly executive leadership team meetings, there are those who speak frequently and those who are quiet. They wish to be heard but perhaps have been afraid to bring up controversial things—issues with other departments or even with me. I solved that by rotating the leadership of our weekly meetings, so those who are reluctant to speak up feel more confident to voice their views by setting the agenda.

For example, when we set forth aggressive sales goals, some team members failed to buy in. The grumbling got louder until we finally aired the issue out. The skepticism was a wake-up call for me; I realized I needed to explain more clearly how we will achieve these goals through mergers and acquisitions. I work *on* the business more, while they work *in* the business.

I also encourage my direct reports to speak straight in one-on-one meetings. As a leader, I'm criticized for sometimes trying to take on too much and not involving my team in the decision-making process. Although I'm not completely cured, I now do a much better job of sharing pertinent information regarding my various "expand our borders" projects.

One of my millennial employees who has worked with me since 2012 never fails to tell it like it is. She speaks straight from her heart, with an eye for detail that is the envy of many. Even though there are 45 years between us, she tells me the truth. Sometimes it hurts my ego, but I take heed and listen.

When you encourage team members to speak straight, you're empowering them to stand up for the values that are important to you and your company.

Tracy Vessillo, president of Florida's Puff 'n Stuff Catering, tells a story that happened when he was visiting a fuel company in Texas—a business that must take safety standards seriously. Tracy was on his phone while riding on the escalator. When he got to the bottom, a maintenance worker stopped him: "Excuse me, sir, but phones must be put away while on the escalator so no one gets hurt."

The worker was mopping the floor, but approaching an executive in a suit didn't intimidate him. He knew it was his job to impart the company culture.

Similarly, at Puff 'n Stuff, serving high-quality food is part of the culture. If someone on the sales team is at an event and sees something that's not up to the company's usual standards, he or she knows to bring it to the attention of the chefs in the kitchen. The same goes company-wide, no matter the department, with team members at all levels encouraged to give helpful feedback. No drama, no hurt feelings. Just everyone working together to create the best experiences possible.

HONOR YOUR COMMITMENTS—EVEN WHEN IT'S DIFFICULT

In my younger days, I would sometimes make the mistake of saying, "This will be an easy party." Inevitably, what I thought would be a slow-pitch softball turned into a nasty curveball.

In off-premise catering, nothing is easy. We are the Navy SEALs of the hospitality world, swooping in and transforming blank canvases into weddings and events that people will remember for the rest of their lives. We're swimming through uncharted waters, hoping to make it safely to shore.

Clients expect us to honor our commitment to delight their guests, regardless of last-minute surprises. And we do—that's what has made my team and me successful. There will always be unexpected requests during an event. Here are a few we've had sprung on us last-minute:

- "One of my guests needs a kosher meal!"
- "We forgot to tell you that we need one bottle of Johnny Walker Blue on the bar."
- "The bride's father will only drink a rare Scotch whisky."

Then there are the logistical challenges that no one can predict—a locked gate at a venue; an unexpected downpour (after the client refused to pay for a tent on standby); a truck breaking down on the way to a wedding; soup spilling in the back of the delivery van.

At my own son's wedding, the limo transporting the elderly guests broke down as it arrived at the wedding location, Vizcaya Museum and Gardens. Fortunately, they only had to walk a short way down a shaded walkway to the magnificent venue on the shores of Biscayne Bay.

But there's no room for excuses on a wedding day. We have one shot to pull it off, to fulfill the commitment to our client to "wow" their guests. And we do; that's our culture.

The same is true for the commitments we make to our team members, who are my internal customers. There's little worse than telling a team member that you will do something and then dropping the ball. That's a surefire way to ruin morale. Clearly, there are times when you promise a team member something, and due to circumstances beyond your control, you cannot honor that commitment. At least explain to your employee why you couldn't deliver on your promise and assure him or her that this is not the end ... circumstances may change in the future.

MAKE QUALITY PERSONAL

Somerset Maugham said, "If you refuse to accept anything but the best, you very often get it." This goes for both you and your team members. Just because people are happy on the job does not mean they are engaged. Learn ways to spot the difference—and how to inspire team members to take pride in their work and make quality personal.

Engaged team members consistently work on ways to improve themselves, their work, and the company. My team members are always making suggestions for improvement, and some take the initiative to "just do it" and wait for approval ... and perhaps the occasional disapproval. (After all, sometimes it's easier to ask for forgiveness than permission.)

Sean Sweeney with CP Communications in Florida is a quality fanatic, who says that quality employees practice "A+ness." Getting an "A" in school was good, he says, but an "A+" represents a totally different level. These A+ers are the cream of the crop because they simply won't accept anything but the very best from themselves and their co-workers.

"Quality is contagious," says Sean. "There's a positive peer pressure when everyone is working at their highest level. These types of people have an overdeveloped excellence muscle."

In my business, when I tour my commissary, I admire the way my team members take particular pride in each item, whether it's a perfectly seared steak or a painstakingly handcrafted hors d'oeuvre.

My warehouse teams practice a form of Six Sigma to achieve loading perfection. When something at an off-premise event is missing, chaos ensues; team members scramble for replacements, running to nearby stores and placing frantic calls to other vendors.

To avoid this, our teams produce a post-event review that details what went right with the delivery and what went wrong. The goal is to learn from our errors to ensure a perfect delivery.

Even so, our executive leadership team meets each Wednesday to find ways to improve the quality of our company. We also make sure to give credit to our team members for quality work. We never want to be the type of company where our employees say: "Doing a good job here is like wetting our pants in a dark suit. We each get a warm feeling, but no one else seems to notice!"

Strive for perfection. Pursuing it will result in excellence, followed by growth.

CHAPTER 6
CUSTOMER RELATIONS
HOW TO TAME THE BRIDEZILLA (AND OTHER UNREASONABLE CUSTOMERS)

Ritz-Carlton's motto is, "We are ladies and gentlemen serving ladies and gentlemen." We strive to emulate that, but what happens when the bride is no lady, and the groom is no gentleman?

No matter what you do for a living, you must deal with unreasonable, rude customers who fail to treat you with respect and dignity. In my business, we call the worst of these a "bridezilla." True bridezillas are few and far between, thankfully. But difficult customers aren't.

How can you satisfy such customers—and if you can't, what then? Following are some of the "bridezilla" traits that we and some of our catering colleagues have encountered over the years, along with some tips on how to tame them. If you can transform these challenging clients into satisfied, grateful customers, you'll find opportunities for growth and excellence.

TREATING STAFF MEMBERS POORLY

Sometimes, bridezillas and their ilk can be spotted by their "me, me, me" attitude. Yes, a wedding is about the couple getting married—but that doesn't mean everyone else can be treated like dirt.

Lisa Dupar, owner of Lisa Dupar Catering in Redmond, Washington, had an inkling about a client's bridezilla nature while watching her interact with her own bridal party. "She was just so mean, it was unbelievable," recalls Lisa. But she and her team didn't understand the full scope of the bride and her family's disregard for other people until the night of the big event.

The wedding took place at the bride's parents' residence on one of the San Juan Islands, which necessitated Lisa and her staff traveling three hours from Seattle. For the most part it went well, with a couple of red flags—there was supposed to be an outdoor tent set up for the catering kitchen (there wasn't), and Lisa was told her staff members couldn't use the restrooms rented for the guests OR go in the house (Lisa put her foot down against that ridiculous decree).

Just after the married couple took off in a helicopter for their honeymoon, Lisa and her team were abruptly told that they had 10 minutes to vacate the garage—where the scullery was set up—before the lights were turned off and it was locked up (apparently, there was a baby in the house who needed to sleep). Unable to clean up in the dark, the catering staffers called it a day, with plans to come back to finish in the morning.

That's when the biggest discourtesy was discovered. The mother of the bride had said during the planning process that she would take care of the staffers' accommodations. After a 16-hour workday, the women were sent off to one address and the men to another. "At the sleazy hotel that was arranged for the women, we discovered upon arrival that the mother of the bride planned for us to share beds with each other," says Lisa. "When I asked the front desk for more rooms, the man behind the counter pointed to his own bedroom behind check-in and told me I could share his room with him." Needless to say, she declined.

Exhausted, after getting to a room with a filthy bathroom, Lisa and her lead server, Shelly, crawled into the bed they had to share to try to get some shut-eye. "With the lights out, Shelly said, 'Damn, I never thought I'd have to sleep with my boss!' We both had a laugh, and I deeply appreciated her humor in that moment," says Lisa.

When they met for breakfast the next morning, Lisa found out from the men that their "rooms" were at a campground with bunk beds and no bathrooms.

Lisa says she learned two hard lessons during that event 20 years ago: "We have told people we are not the caterer for them when there are enough red flags. I'm never doing that to my staff again, ever. If we're not being treated kindly, there's not enough money in the world.

"And we have never let a client arrange our accommodations since."

TRYING TO GET A FREEBIE

Business owners and managers must remember that before a sale, you are in charge, and after the sale, your customer is in charge. Cash is king; be sure to get enough of it in advance, so if things head south with your client, you are protected. Remember that even credit card payments can be disputed.

And sometimes you'll encounter someone who never had any intention of paying—like Chris Villard did with the "Trying to Get a Freebie" Bridezilla.

Chris is now the general manager of a catering company in Atlanta, but when he was with another catering firm, he dealt with a bride who terrorized his entire team.

It all started with a couple who weren't paying their bills. By the Wednesday before the Saturday wedding, the bride and groom hadn't put down a deposit or made any payments. Chris let them know the wedding would be canceled if they didn't pay up. On Friday afternoon, they finally came through with a check at 4 p.m.—which meant Chris's team was unable to deposit it immediately.

The groom signed off on the venue setup: "He said it looked great, and we got a signature. But as soon as the ceremony was over and they were shuttled to the event space, the bride started complaining about her bouquet that we had done. Then she took our floral assistant around and basically told every one of her guests, 'This is the [expletive] that ruined my wedding!'"

What followed was a full-blown tantrum by the bride, in which she screamed at the entire staff, cursing and complaining about every aspect of the wedding. Chris was called over from another event and tried to pacify her. "I asked the bride, 'What can we do at this moment to fix things?'" he says. "But she just kept screaming obscenities and yelling at me."

So, to protect them from further abuse, Chris sent his staff outside and said he would text them when he needed something. "It was a horrible experience for our team, and it was just outrageous," he says.

Even after the wedding, the nightmare wasn't over. The bridezilla stopped payment on her check for $13,000. Chris's company immediately filed a lawsuit for $25,000, and when all was said and done, the bride was forced to pay $36,000—covering even the catering firm's lawyer fees.

"They were trying to get away without paying for a wedding," says Chris, who believes his company won the case because they had proof on their side—photos documenting the event setup, the husband's signature approving it, and even screenshots of the bride bragging about her florals on Instagram, after complaining about them in person. "It was an exciting victory for us, even though it was painful."

In catering and many other businesses, taking personal checks—and delivering the goods and services before the check clears—is a dangerous practice. In my company, if we're dealing with a last-minute-paying bride, we must receive a cashier's check or cash. Personal checks are only worth the paper they are written on.

HAVING CHAMPAGNE TASTE ON A BEER BUDGET

I hear this all the time: "Bill, we're on a very tight budget, so be gentle with your pricing."

"OK, I understand," I reply. "What is your budget? Perhaps we can work something out."

And then I often hear, "Bill, we're not sure yet."

Well, well, well. Houston, we have a problem. How can a couple plan a wedding without a budget of some sort?

My team and I help clients in all price ranges, tapping into a variety of catering resources—from budget brands to ultra-luxury experiences. However, I realized early in my career that most people have no idea what catering costs. After all, many people have never hired a caterer.

Some clients come to us with prices from their favorite restaurants, forgetting that in off-premise catering we need to build a kitchen and a dining area, prepare and serve the food, and then break down the event in less than an hour. We often must provide the serving staff, chinaware, flatware, stemware, tables, chairs, and linens. For many clients, we also handle the florals, music, valet … You name it, we do it.

When it all adds up, some clients go into sticker shock.

Then they tell us why *they* should get a lower price than our other customers. But how do you politely respond when a client's reasoning is, frankly, insulting?

One socialite client, well known in Miami, called me and told me that she wanted filet mignon in lieu of chicken for her party on Indian Creek Island, the "Billionaire Bunker" that's home to Jeff Bezos, and Jared Kushner and Ivanka Trump. I was happy to hear that until she told me she wanted it for the same price. I gave her a firm "no," and suggested she go with another caterer. She finally agreed to the higher price, and we are still on good terms to this day.

Here are some of the most memorable ways our clients have told us they want catering on the cheap (without saying "cheap"). And here's how we've learned to pacify them and still make a profit.

"A lot of important people will be at my party."
That's wonderful. We've served many important people, including four U.S. presidents, Pope John Paul II, Billy Graham, Jerry Seinfeld, Robert Kraft, Reese Witherspoon, the list goes on. ... Know that we will treat all your guests as VIPs.

"This will be good exposure for you."
We perform at our best when we are fully staffed, so we wouldn't be making the best impression if we had to lower our service levels.

"It's just a simple, casual party."
I've learned over the years that no party is "simple," which is why we never cut corners on staffing or food, and we charge accordingly.

"We're not out to impress anyone."
Neither are we. We aim to delight our guests, not impress them. I've seen many events sour when hosts are determined to impress—i.e., show off—rather than make sure their guests are having a good time.

"The kids are paying for their wedding themselves."
Oh, that's great. Could you put me in touch with them? We like to communicate with our clients directly.

"These women don't eat anything. They eat like birds."
I'm tempted to ask, "What kind of bird—a canary or an ostrich?" But instead, I explain that service accounts for most of the cost of an event. So even if you opt for small portions, you're still paying for the service. Some clients say, "Well, what if we have a buffet-style event; won't that cut down on service?" I respond, "It can lower the service cost slightly, but our food is so good, your guests will be coming back to the buffet for seconds and thirds!"

"Our friends don't drink much."
This excuse has echoed in my head many times as I ran to the liquor store in the middle of an event because we were on the verge of running out of booze. "We want your guests to be delighted," we explain, "so we always provide a fully stocked beverage selection."

"We don't need much service. We like to do things ourselves."
Our servers arrive early to set up, are sometimes called to help in the kitchen, work the entire event, and are the last people to leave, after stacking tables and chairs. You'll be working during the entire event. Don't you want to spend time with your family and friends, and be a guest at your own party?

"We're a nonprofit organization."
I'd like to respond, "Well, we're a for-profit organization." Instead, I say that we are happy to work with worthwhile nonprofits. We often work for lower margins in exchange for benefits such as database information, comp tickets, and—most important—free marketing, such as our name on banners, programs, etc. Make sure you specify in advance what your company will be getting in exchange for providing your services at a discount.

"I was in your business, and I know all the tricks."
Catering is an art and a profession. Caterers who pull tricks on their customers won't be in business for very long, and I've been catering since the late 1960s.

"Can I bring my own meat?"
Some ask this in jest. But we do allow this if the meat comes from licensed, reputable sources. For example, in South Florida, clients may have contacts with local fishermen, who can provide them with stone crabs. We crack and serve, giving the customers credit on their invoice for what we would have paid for the crabs.

Budget-conscious customers will also appreciate any tips you can give them to save money. Here are a few I share:

- Book your event on a weeknight and during the off-season. In South Florida, a Tuesday night in July will be priced considerably less than a Saturday night in December.
- If you're planning a wedding, attend bridal shows and take advantage of the special offers.

- A simple buffet with low-cost foods will save money on staffing.
- Rather than passed hors d'oeuvres during the cocktail hour, substitute with platters and dips placed on tables to save on staffing costs.
- Consider booking a food truck. They're fun and economical.
- Instead of paying to rent chinaware, flatware, and glassware, opt for disposable serving ware for casual parties.
- Have you considered drop-off catering? It's a cost-conscious choice for a casual event. The caterer leaves the food but doesn't provide service, though the client can hire a server or two to help.

BEING A SCHOOLYARD BULLY

Some clients never outgrew their schoolyard bullying days. They throw their weight around, acting as if their status as paying customers enables them to treat you and everyone on your staff with disrespect.

Those of us in the hospitality business are especially susceptible to this abuse, as we are trained to serve with a smile. We tend to bend over backwards, perform somersaults, and go out on a limb to please this type of client. Sometimes, however, we have to say, "Enough is enough!"

One big-bucks bully refused to listen to our advice regarding the installation of a tent and dance floor over a pool for a party at his Miami Beach mansion. Rain was predicted. We gave him a deadline, which he ignored. Finally, the day before his event, he ordered us to find a tent and pool cover for him. On a busy Miami weekend, tents don't appear out of the woodwork.

Our usual tent supplier does not cover swimming pools, so we needed to contract another supplier. We rented the tent and pool cover from them, but the last-minute installation had us at our wits' end. The company forgot to bring rain gutters and walls. Meanwhile, the client berated the men installing the tent and yelled at my team, complaining that we were too slow, and he didn't like the tent.

In any business there will be unruly clients like these. Sometimes, going the extra mile for them can backfire, as it did with us. We allowed the client to get away with ignoring a deadline, which resulted in extra stress for my team. While the party ended up being a success, and the client was pleased, we learned a lesson—stick to our processes, which were put in place for a reason.

Most corporate clients are professional, organized, and easy to work with. Yet there are exceptions—and one stands out as a classic. Our disorganized client from the medical field was planning multiple-day events, totaling in the low six figures. He was under the watchful eyes of his superiors, which was a clue that he needed close supervision for these important events.

My team went above and beyond attempting to please him, even with last-minute requests. Our event manager personally made the breakfast breads to ensure they were safe for an executive with an airborne nut allergy. She drove all over town to find the specific 10-inch-square plastic plates that he requested, and frantically sourced last-minute ice cream treats.

"In all my years of catering, I've never had a client like him!" said Elizabeth Silverman, sales and event manager from my Lovables Catering & Kitchen division. "No matter what we did, it didn't seem as if it were enough. Quite frankly, I just wanted to get paid and never see him again!"

Even getting paid was tricky with this client. He failed to acknowledge our invoices, ignoring our calls, texts, and emails. He didn't even submit them to accounts payable until five weeks after the events. It took over two months to get paid, causing cash flow issues for me and tons of frustrating moments for my team, who were waiting for their commissions.

There are a few lessons from these stories:

1. Make sure you're paid in advance.

2. If you can spot these types of clients early, run for the hills, and suggest they do business elsewhere!
3. But if you missed the early-warning signs and are stuck, charge extra for your trouble.

Catering guru Mike Roman called these charges "aggravation charges." Every time a client makes an unreasonable demand, we accommodate, but price it accordingly—and add in some extra for aggravation.

My wife Terry has learned these lessons well. She proved it in the early '90s, when we were invited to do a food tasting at the aptly named Club Hell. This short-lived nightclub on South Beach was owned by German developer Thomas Kramer, who played a big role in the redevelopment of that legendary stretch of Miami Beach.

After my partner, Bill Hendrich, and my most senior team member, Thelma Corea, prepared the food outside in the blazing sun, we served Kramer the perfectly cooked and seasoned mini beef sliders. He tasted them, made a face, and told Terry that he needed to bring his German chefs to Miami to teach us how to cook.

Without missing a beat, Terry responded, "I think you *will* need your own cooks, Mr. Kramer, because we are out of here!"

While Bill, Thelma, and I were getting ready to serve the next course, Terry was gathering up our utensils and platters from inside the club. She then stormed out the back door and announced, "We're leaving!" The planner who introduced us to Kramer pleaded with us to stay, but there was no way in hell Terry was staying at Club Hell after the owner insulted us all.

Take it from Terry: There are times when you need to walk away from what could be a lucrative contract because the potential payoff is not worth being demeaned by a client.

MAKING UNREASONABLE DEMANDS

Training sessions in many corporations teach that "the customer is always right." As professionals, you and I know this is not true.

Sometimes the customer is right. But sometimes the customer makes unreasonable demands that must be met with patience, tact, a smile, and a touch of humor.

We've had to talk clients out of:

- Making table centerpieces out of cages with live birds.
- Shining bright lights on the buffet florals so that leaves, petals, and seeds droop into the food.
- Placing soup as a first offering for guests in a buffet line, setting up a dangerous juggling act.
- Jamming so many tables into an event space, alongside strolling musicians, that wait staff can barely serve the guests.
- Placing buckets of beer on each table, which goes against safe service rules—and makes it easy for minors to illegally access alcohol.

The team at Blue Plate Catering in Madison, Wisconsin, went above and beyond trying to please a couple who critiqued everything they sampled. At their first tasting for the wedding's station menu, "they wanted to try every single item on every single station, down to the garbanzo beans," recalls David Porto, Blue Plate's general manager. Then they flew in both of their mothers for a second tasting, and Blue Plate had four critics on their hands.

"There was not a single item on our menu that they didn't make an adjustment to," says David—even requesting an adjustment to the latticework on the mini cherry pies. "They said, 'The garlic mashed potatoes are super great, but we want more butter and less salt.' In 19 years, I'd never had anyone want to change anything about our mashed potatoes!"

When clients are being especially difficult, it's helpful to extend some empathy, notes David. "While catering is something we do every day, this is two families coming together for the first time," he says, adding that brides and grooms often feel immense pressure to pull off an event that will please everyone involved. "Remember that fighting fire with fire won't work. Be the calm in the storm, and accept all their feedback." When a testy email arrives, walk away before responding, he advises.

Although the high-maintenance couple caused a lot of headaches for David and his staff, his affable approach paid off. Both families were thrilled with the event. "We are so happy with how everything turned out," the bride wrote to David, adding that she especially enjoyed the process of designing custom menus. (He was tempted to respond, "I'm glad one of us did!" but showed his customary restraint.)

In the 1990s, Bonura Hospitality was working with a couple who wanted to celebrate their daughter's bat mitzvah at their very popular venue Anthony's Pier 9 in Windsor, New York. The girl's mother insisted on perfection and asked for a seemingly endless list of guarantees. Owner Joe Bonura acquiesced to all the demands until the client said: "And you have to guarantee me that there won't be a single piece of paper on the floor in the ladies room."

At that point, Joe tore up the contract and said, "You know what, I can't make you happy." He asked them to take their business elsewhere.

The woman's husband pleaded for Joe to reconsider, saying he would take care of his wife and assuring Joe that he knew the party would be great. It was—the couple came back for their younger daughter's bat mitzvah and, years later, for both of their weddings. After the second wedding, the praise was effusive, says Mike Bonura, Joe's son, now a partner at Bonura Hospitality. The bride's parents told him that the catering had been perfect.

"The moral of the story is to know your worth," says Mike. "Sometimes, when the client can't have something, then it becomes what they really want, and some of the toughest people to deal with become some of the easier people to deal with."

One bridezilla who thought she was Martha Stewart pushed me to the limit. Her wedding took place at the Charles Deering Estate in South Dade, a historic venue on the bay with fabulous views. Inside is a small ballroom where seating at round tables works best for maximum capacity. Mini-Martha concocted a seating chart using larger tables, arranged to fit 60 of her victims (I mean guests). I said, "No, it won't work." She left in a huff to see her florist, who I knew very well.

Later that day the florist called me and regaled me with stories about how my bride was trashing me.

Bad vibes coming from mini-Martha is not the way to create a wonderful experience. So I called one of my former team members, John McPhee from Joy Wallace Catering. I explained the situation, and John agreed to cater the event, which was only five days away.

Quickly, I called the bride and told her I felt very uncomfortable doing the catering considering the bad vibes. "I've arranged for another caterer to work with you," I said, "and I will refund your deposit!" That's how eager I was to be done with this client. I made my call on Wednesday and her wedding was the following Sunday.

Surprisingly, she acquiesced to my ultimatum, hired a bridal planner to help her, and paid me in full. The wedding went off without a hitch—except for the rain at her ceremony, which brought with it thousands of mosquitoes. A nuisance for a nuisance?

MEDDLING AND MICROMANAGING

Self-appointed experts with little experience, and perhaps a title, are difficult to deal with. These come in all varieties: the clients themselves, wedding consultants, event planners, corporate administrators, fundraisers, or those who think they're experts because they've been in the business for many years. (Many are too proud to keep learning or to listen to those from the next generation.) They cause headaches and confusion, and they can impact your bottom line.

Great event planners—and I've worked with many of them—enhance the couple's experience and support the caterer and other vendors. But there are outliers. We've dealt with planners who steal ideas from one vendor and share them with the competition; underestimate the number of guaranteed guests and drastically increase the guest count the day before the event; schedule tastings for their client with every caterer in town, which wastes a lot of time for all involved; tell us no vendor meals are needed and then demand them at the wedding; and expect us to take care of details on the day of the event that are their responsibility.

Planners who've refused to listen to my team's expertise have ruined many events. One scheduled fireworks along the bay at Miami's Vizcaya Museum and Gardens, while failing to notice pelicans floating restfully on the water. But not for long! With the first explosion, the birds panicked, flying over the heads of the guests while drenching them with bay water and pelican droppings.

Whether you're a customer or a vendor, don't rely on social media when hiring an event planner—or any middleman in any industry. Get reviews from other customers, and remember they can make or break a project.

And then there are the micromanagers, who drive all business owners crazy. Picture this: The party was in full swing, with all the guests out on the dance floor, having the time of their lives. But the micromanager cut the music off to adhere to a schedule. Another 15 minutes of music would not have made a difference, but the micromanager couldn't see the big picture and attempted to serve the main course when guests weren't ready to eat.

Setting clear expectations at the beginning of the relationship will help you deal with micromanagers. Tell the client what they can expect from you and what you will need from them. Project management tools and software allow clients to track the progress themselves to give them a sense of control. In my firm we use Tripleseat software, which allows online access for our clients. They can track the event's progress 24/7/365.

You should also establish a clear chain of command. We've had bridal clients with too many cooks in the kitchen—the bride, both moms, the wedding planner, and friends all giving their advice and asking staff to complete tasks. This becomes complicated because we wish to please everyone and delight all the guests.

We tell couples that they—along with their wedding planner—should make the decisions. Moms and friends can deal directly with the planner, who in turn will communicate with us. Our time is valuable, and this method saves time and cuts down on confusion.

Every business has these issues, where too many people have a voice. One way to deal with this is to schedule a private meeting with the bill-payers and explain that while everyone's opinion is important, their decision will be the final decision.

To sum up, demanding and unruly customers come with the territory in any business. Yet there are strategies you can employ to effect the best outcome:

- Stay calm, cool, and collected. Patience and empathy will defuse tension.
- Listen to the client while empathizing with their thoughts and feelings.
- Be firm when setting boundaries.
- Work toward a mutually beneficial solution.
- Know when to walk away or call management, security, and—if necessary—the police.
- Document everything in case legal action could follow.

CHAPTER 7
QUALITY FIRST
THE BEST ADVERTISING IS ON THE END OF THE FORK

I'VE HAD A MANTRA FOR over five decades, though it wasn't coined by me: "The best advertising is on the end of the fork!"

Those words were often spoken by John Mossman, owner of Mossman's Catering in Bakersfield, California. And he meant that no matter how good your marketing is, no matter how many ads you run or Instagram photos you post, if your food isn't good, you're not going to make it. If your service isn't good, you're not going to make it.

And if they are good, your marketing job is a whole heck of a lot easier!

While the importance of quality seems obvious, sometimes it's harder to grasp how to obtain it and maintain it.

My dear friend, retired restaurant manager Chuck Mercurio, had 10 Commandments for Running a Business. Here's one: "Good enough" isn't accepted. Never settle for "It's OK"!

Compromise is for politics and salary negotiations, not for your products or services.

GO THE EXTRA MILE

Here's a lesson I've learned over and over again in my career: Have a plan; have a back-up plan; and be prepared to wing it—or, in this case, floor it—when all else fails.

PLATING UP PROFITS

Whenever I drive by downtown Miami's DuPont Building, my heart beats a little faster remembering the anxiety of one unforgettable wedding. The building—an Art Deco skyscraper nicknamed the Rockefeller Center of the South and the first air-conditioned building south of Atlanta—was originally home to Florida National Bank. The Ressler family purchased it in 1991, and in 2002 they turned it into a special events venue—one that would host the wedding of the owner's son.

The Ressler ceremony was held on the other side of Flagler Street in the Olympia Theater, built in 1926 during the silent movie era. Designed to resemble a Moorish-style Spanish courtyard, the theater has hosted such cultural icons as Elvis Presley, B.B. King, Luciano Pavarotti, and Etta James under its ceiling of stars.

But on this Saturday night it was decked out for the Ressler wedding.

After post-ceremony cocktails and passed bites, the guests were invited across Flagler Street to the main reception in the DuPont Building.

But how would they cross Flagler Street in style? The Resslers arranged to have this main east-west artery at the center of Miami closed to traffic for an hour, as guests strolled on a red carpet across the street into the DuPont's main entrance, where—with champagne flutes in hand—they rode the spectacular escalators to the second floor for more drinks, bites, and then the sumptuous feast.

For us, there was one caveat: Six kosher meals were needed, which we ordered in advance. And it was my job to pick them up at 8 p.m. at Temple Emanu-El on Miami Beach. Dinner was to be served promptly at 9:30.

Not a problem. I always allow extra time in case of emergencies. Arriving at the temple at around 7:45, I called the kitchen and was told the meals had not arrived from a sister temple in Hollywood, about an hour to the north.

Not willing to wait, I jumped back in the car and raced up I-95. With little traffic and a heavy foot, I made it there in about 30 minutes. After finally locating the kitchen, I asked one of the three cooks: "Where are my meals? I'm here to pick them up."

"Bad news, my friend," came the reply. "The mashgiach isn't here yet, and the walk-in cooler is locked."

"When will he arrive?"

"We're not sure, we called him a couple of times."

Heart racing, I noticed that the six settings of kosher-prepped china and flatware were there. At least that was on point.

"Any suggestions?" I asked them. "What would you do if you were me?" That's always a good question to ask—even if you're part of the problem, you can be part of the solution.

After learning there was a kosher restaurant at Williams Island, I raced out with my plates and flatware. I dialed the restaurant and placed my order along the way while weaving in and out of the southbound I-95 traffic at breakneck speed.

What speed limit? I couldn't let the Resslers down. I'd catered on a yacht at Williams Island before, so I knew the back delivery entrance to the restaurant. After parking illegally outside to avoid the five-minute walk from the main lot, I rushed in.

"Where are my meals?" I asked.

"They're not ready!" someone responded. "We were waiting for you!"

I didn't say anything about placing my order already and giving them my Amex. I've learned it's best not to get smart or cute when playing an away game in unfamiliar territory. I was not in control of the cooking; they were.

It was 9 p.m. when the meals were ready. I'm sure I hit 100 mph on I-95, but I pulled up in front of the DuPont in the nick of time. And the Resslers didn't learn about the near misadventure until years later.

Delivering quality, freshly cooked food can be much trickier than it seems, but by literally going the extra miles that evening, my clients and all their guests dined on crispy chilled salads and hot-off-the-grill New York strip steaks.

DEFINE YOUR CUSTOMERS BEFORE DEFINING YOUR QUALITY STANDARDS

Who are your customers?

You must define your market before defining your quality measures and price points.

For example, in the restaurant business, are we talking fast food, casual dining, or fine dining? Each one has its own quality measures based upon the price a customer is willing to pay.

My team and I are innovators in this arena, offering catering services at varying price points, under different brands. At each level, quality is important—but the standards for quality differ based on the price the customer is willing to pay. Think filet mignon versus meatloaf.

My top brand, Bill Hansen Catering, delivers not only high-quality food but unparalleled service. Sometimes, if the client's budget permits, we schedule one server for every five guests. Alexander, my midscale brand at a lower price, offers fine food quality, but with fewer servers and frills. My budget brand, at the lowest price point, is Lovables Catering & Kitchen, which serves less expensive food with limited or no service.

Here's what it boils down to: **Quality is in the eye of the beholder.** Without understanding your customer, you can't understand how they gauge quality.

For example, if you were dining with Daniel Boulud at Daniel, renowned for its world-class cuisine, wine cellar, and gracious hospitality, and the waiter served you a Whopper, you would walk out without saying goodbye. However, after missing breakfast and lunch and no time for dinner, a Whopper might seem like the best food you've ever tasted. Clearly, convenience and pricing lowered your quality standards. Your evaluative criteria changed based upon your current needs.

Understanding your customers' needs and what they're willing to pay is critical for developing quality standards.

BE CONSISTENT

A hotel guest called room service and ordered the following: raw bacon, gritty hash browns, two sunny-side-up eggs—one crispy and overcooked, and the other upside-down with no yolk visible—a cup of lukewarm coffee, and curdled cream.

The room service attendant huffily replied, "There is no way we can serve a breakfast like that!" The guest responded, "Yes, you can. That's what you sent to my room yesterday!"

That joke always gets a chuckle, and it's easy to understand why—as a consumer, whatever your experience is at a business or a restaurant, you'll expect to get that same experience the next time you visit.

And that's why quality must be consistent.

Have you ever been inside an Aldi? It's the fastest-growing grocery store chain in America. One of Aldi's core values is consistency. When you visit one of their approximately 2,400 locations in the U.S., you'll find pretty much the same layout and the same products—although the stores will stock up to 10 percent of items based on regional tastes. To ensure consistency of their products, Aldi does frequent testing—the company says it taste-tested more than 30,000 products in 2023. Aldi's commitment to consistency is one reason why it's winning the grocery wars.

Have you ever dined at a restaurant, loved the food and service, and couldn't wait to go back again? But when you returned to the same eatery, the service was sloppy, and the food was barely edible? It happens all the time—and it's even harder to maintain consistency in the catering world. In catering, it's not easy to replicate quality when we're cooking outside, under a tent, with portable cooking equipment that sometimes doesn't work while standing in the middle of a growing puddle of water. Rookie caterers often fail under these punishing circumstances.

I recall one wedding three decades ago at Vizcaya. I returned to the event while hors d'oeuvres were being served after retrieving a missing item from my commissary. As I approached the venue, I could see my culinary team rushing around frantically. Seems the rental oven had failed to work—a very big problem! Yet my team members jumped into action, loading food into hot boxes to be cooked with canned fuel. (This is called cave cooking, which is commonplace in many museums and galleries that prohibit the use of propane on their property.) Against the odds, we delivered a quality hot meal—and our client and guests never saw us sweat.

INSPECT FOR GREATNESS INSTEAD OF EXPECTING GREATNESS

Taste, taste, and then taste again. Top chefs taste their food before they serve it. That's one way they control the quality.

My corporate executive chef, Dewey LoSasso, has tasting spoons stocked everywhere throughout the kitchen. "Tasting is like breathing," he says. "It's a constant thing." Food prepped the day before an event is tasted again before it goes out the door. Items like coleslaw may taste different hours after they're made so retasting is mandatory.

"Teaching tasting food is one of the hardest things I do," says Dewey. "I sometimes let a cook make something with seasoning. I take a taste and set the spoon aside. Then I show him how to season the dish. Then we taste my dish and his dish. That's when my cook gets it."

In his book *Who Says Elephants Can't Dance*, which chronicles how he turned around IBM, Louis Gerstner said, "People do what you inspect, not what you expect."

In other words, you'll never have a great product if you just hope for it. You must put systems in place that define expectations—and systems that measure whether those expectations have been met.

Of course, in catering it takes more than great food to be a star. We all have warehouses full of cooking equipment and serving vessels, and what we don't have we rent. But all it takes is one missing item when we're cooking somewhere remote—like we've done in the middle of the Everglades only accessible by airboat—to ruin an event, regardless of how good the food tastes.

Tables, chairs, linen, china, flatware, and stemware must be carefully checked before and after arriving at a venue. Once when we rented black wooden folding chairs for an event, they arrived covered with chips and scuffs. I demanded that the rental firm come to my venue and paint each chair. Another time, in a fit of rage, I took a rented table with broken legs and threw it into Biscayne Bay. It sank to the bottom … never to frustrate another caterer again. I don't do that anymore, but my team is trained to inspect everything at least once and sometimes twice.

Here's an example: When arriving at an event and checking the dining area, I make sure that each chair brushes the tablecloth at a 90-degree angle to the place setting instead of being pushed under the table, which moves the linen. After setup is complete, and my staff has a meal and our pre-event pep talk, we often find that musicians, planners, and other vendors have moved the chairs during their setup. So we perform a second check just before guests enter the dining area to make sure everything is picture-perfect.

Here's a quick way to know whether the restaurant you're dining in has a good quality-management system in place: Check the salt and pepper shakers. Are they clean, filled to the brim, and positioned uniformly on each table? If so, you probably chose wisely (by the way, salt is usually placed to the right of the pepper because most people are right-handed and salt is requested more than pepper).

Double- and triple-checking our inventory prior to leaving our commissary and when we arrive at the event is part of the quality control process. Among the many things we check for are cleanliness; missing parts for coffee makers and other equipment; proper packing in the required shipping containers; and how the items are packed in the vehicle to avoid breaking or spilling.

We learned the necessity of the final check the hard way. In my early catering years, we once forgot the cocktail sauce and needed to make an emergency run to our commissary to retrieve it. After my van skidded to a stop back at our temporary kitchen, we opened the door only to discover all the red sauce seeping out. Seems the five-gallon container of cocktail sauce wasn't properly secured. Never again!

As I like to say, catering is not rocket science, but it is an exact science.

Another way we test quality is by taking photos of each dish we serve. In that way, we can ensure that food is presented at the event in the same way it was presented at the tasting. After all, preparing food for two guests is completely different than serving the same food to 200 guests in a venue that's not home base. Yet our clients will expect the food that they're paying for to look like it did when they tasted it. Before any plate leaves our off-premise catering kitchen, an expediter checks it against a posted photo of how the dish should look, and makes sure rims are sauce-free.

Each menu item must adhere to predefined standards. For example, we generally serve our filets medium rare—tender enough to chew easily with a light-pink center and charred brown exterior. Portion sizes range from 4 to 8 ounces.

We also check the staff in a lineup prior to the guests' arrival. Some minor discrepancies can be remedied on-site with an iron, lint brush, hair spray, etc. If a staff member isn't dressed properly, however, we send them home. Since this can be risky and leave us short-handed, for large events when we are using staff members who work for us infrequently, we schedule extra staff in case there are problems. And if we do end up short-staffed, I'll try to incentivize the remaining workers with a small bonus for their extra efforts.

REMEMBER: QUALITY STARTS AT THE BACK DOOR

You can have quality control processes in place for every aspect of your business, but if you're not extending that level of attention to your vendors, it could all fall apart. In other words, what's going out the front door won't be any good if you have garbage coming in the back door.

At 81 years old, Joe Bonura still makes weekly trips to hand-select fish and produce from local markets for the New York company he founded, Bonura Hospitality. He's accompanied on the outings by his 25-year-old grandson, ensuring that top-notch ingredients will remain a priority for the family-run business. "It's being hands-on and making sure that we get the right stuff," says partner Mike Bonura, Joe's son. "You want to try to save money wherever you can, but you can't sacrifice quality while doing it."

When Tracy Vessillo worked as president of Wolfgang Puck Catering, he was impressed by the celebrity chef's devotion to quality. "In our industry, we tend to put profitability pretty high on the priority list, right? But with Wolfgang, it was kind of the opposite," says Tracy. "First came quality. And if we made less money on it, we made less money on it. His name was on it, and he wanted to make sure that his guests were getting nothing but the absolute best."

Vessillo brought that mindset with him when he became president of Puff'n Stuff Catering in Orlando, Tampa, and Jacksonville, Florida. Upon arrival, Tracy gave his chefs some grace on their targeted food costs, encouraging them to focus even more on superior ingredients. Puff'n Stuff already had a reputation for emphasizing quality, but that extra push has paid off in increased revenues.

"Fresh foods are really where it makes a difference," says Tracy, noting that Puff 'n Stuff eschews frozen foods, buys local and organic as much as possible, and makes about 80 percent of its pastries and breads in-house.

Even seemingly little things—like a pad of butter—can impact the guest experience. Puff 'n Stuff presents its butter cut in a rippled wedge and sprinkled with pink Himalayan sea salt. "When you put that on your bread, you're experiencing a better butter," says Tracy. "We get a lot of compliments on our food; that's one thing that always stands out."

At Bill Hansen Catering, we stringently vet our vendors. Before switching to a vendor who may offer a better price or better service, we'll make some test orders and do tastings to ensure we're not sacrificing quality for price. We value long-term relationships, whether they're providing food products, beverages, or other elements necessary to produce a quality event.

For example, Diamonette Party Rental and Over The Top Rental Linens have been my preferred vendors for rental items for decades. Even more important than the quality of their products is their punctual service. An important lesson I learned early in my career is that the best quality product delivered late is useless. It was in the mid-1980s, and our party rental firm—which was providing the china, flatware, glassware, tables, chairs, and linens—delivered the items so late that my client had to help us set up. We finished just as the 300 guests started pouring out from the buses.

Never again did we do business with that company, and we've exclusively relied on Diamonette since that day. Why? Because they arrive when we schedule them. Case closed!

Many don't know this, but the Redland area of South Florida yields some of the best produce in the world. You wouldn't think of Miami-Dade County as agricultural, but it is. We take advantage of seasonal items to incorporate into our recipes, and the quality shows. Just-picked tomatoes from the vine and strawberries from the field greatly enhance the flavor of our dishes.

The closer the relationship you can forge with your vendor partners in business, the better!

GET INVOLVED IN THE NITTY-GRITTY

A friend once ordered a martini at a cocktail lounge in a five-star hotel. It arrived sans olive. When he asked about the missing garnish, the bartender replied, "The olive shipment didn't come in." What a lame excuse! Instead of disappointing the customer with an inferior cocktail, someone could have run to the grocery store less than a quarter of a mile away and brought back a jar of olives.

A manager who walked the floor would have noticed such an omission. It is simply not possible to run a successful small business from behind a desk, reading computer printouts and delegating all tasks. The best are run like a Greek friend of mine runs his restaurant. He is in the kitchen and the dining area scores of times before and during meal service, checking that his Greek specialties are served at the proper temperature and in a timely, professional manner.

One of the most beloved restaurant chains in South Florida is Flanigan's. Their ribs, burgers, and fresh mahi are unbeatable. And when you dine there, you'll notice there's always a manager on the floor, walking from table to table to ensure things are running smoothly.

I have a routine when I arrive at my commissary. After setting down my laptop, I visit each office to say hello—sometimes giving a hug for good measure. From there I walk into the kitchen and pay my regards to each chef and cook, often saying a quick prayer with them. Then I visit the ladies in my cold kitchen, who have been with me for decades. In this way I stay close with my team members, and they know they can come to me with any concerns.

Off-premise catering companies must be managed from the center of the action, whether that's with the guests or preparing food in the kitchen. I call this "management by walking around." Yet there's much more to it than that.

Most times during events I have the attention span of a gnat, jumping from one detail to another. My eye is always roving for anything that's not quite perfect—a burned-out light bulb, a piece of trash on the floor. Once, my supplier sent chair covers that didn't quite fit. Did we tell the client that the uncovered chairs would do? Of course not. When the original supplier was nowhere to be found, we contacted another supplier who delivered covers that were the right size. We said goodbye to the old supplier and have worked with the "savior supplier" for more than 30 years.

One night in the early '90s, while catering an event at Vizcaya for Kraft Foods, we almost didn't serve one of the products the company is best known for—salad dressing!

We always dress the salads at the last minute so they're crisp and not soggy. When my superstar cook Thelma opened the Igloo coolers, she discovered we had forgotten the dressing. That's the bad news. The worse news is that two planners from Kraft were overseeing our kitchen operation.

The good news? My commissary was only five minutes away from Vizcaya.

Thelma and I hopped in my tricked-out 1980 Ford catering van and I peeled out of Vizcaya, ran a red light, and passed on a double line to get to my commissary. The planners were probably in shock, but within 10 minutes we were back, salad dressing in hand.

Another caterer friend was so eager to be hands-on that he showed up to a client's home a week early. As he approached the house with his catering van, equipment, and staff in tow, the caterer started to feel uneasy, as the home was in disarray. When the confused client came to the door, he asked my friend, "What are you doing here? My party is next Saturday!"

Quick on his feet, the caterer responded, "I know that, but we always do a trial run one week before a party!"

Maintaining quality in a small business is a never-ending quest. For over 50 years I've never been totally satisfied with the way things are. I always look for new ways to present food, make food more flavorful, and find better and more efficient ways of doing things.

Astute small business owners need to:

- Obtain feedback from clients and guests regarding products and services.
- Oversee staff to ensure they are performing as directed and as expected.
- Jump in when needed, whatever the task.

Just make sure when you jump in that you're doing it on the right day! And you'll be happy to know that after years of terrorizing my staff with my driving, I now have a full-time driver on hand to ferry me through the highways and byways of South Florida. Be hands-on—but also know your limits!

CHAPTER 8
DEALING WITH ADVERSITY
TURN YOUR LEMONS INTO LEMONADE AND LEMON CAKE

In 2020, life gave the world lemons.

The COVID-19 pandemic closed many businesses, cost many jobs, and killed way too many people. Some folks are still recovering, and some will never be the same.

When all catered events came to a grinding halt due to the shutdown, my business—like many others—had to find a way to survive. We did, emerging from those dark days stronger than ever. We took the lemons the shutdown gave us and made lemonade and lemon cake.

Keep in mind there will always be setbacks, some beyond our control. Savvy business owners and managers—like the ones profiled in this chapter—wrap themselves in a cloak of resiliency, bouncing back from failures and misfortunes with positive attitudes and a deep determination to persevere.

FINDING SWEETNESS WHEN THE WORLD TURNED SOUR

Bill Hansen Catering was flying high in early 2020. Our phones were ringing off the hook, our calendar was jam-packed, and we were on our way to our best year yet. Life was sweet.

Soon, however, everything soured—for us and everyone else in the world.

In March 2020, I spoke at the Catersource + The Special Event Conference and Tradeshow in Las Vegas as the COVID-19 pandemic was starting to sweep across the country. Exhibitors on the tradeshow floor were rattled by the lack of business, as we attendees wondered what the future held. Leaving Las Vegas was like leaving a ghost town. I'll never forget the eerie silence of the Mandalay Bay casino floor, which would soon close for months.

Back in my Miami commissary, while catching up on business, I received news of a troubling omen—one of my competitors had shut her doors. I had just talked with her amazing executive chef a few nights before at Catersource, discussing a possible future collaboration.

Thinking it was just a rumor, I called one of my former team members from the 1980s who worked for this caterer. He had just been told an hour before that he and the rest of the team were terminated. And that included her very talented executive chef.

Although this caterer and I were fierce competitors after she left my employ in the late 1980s, it was distressing to see my former colleagues unemployed with no notice—and it felt like the dominoes were beginning to fall.

Meanwhile, every phone call and email to my offices and commissary contained the words "canceling" or "postponing." Refunds were flying out of my accounts while the cash inflow was nil.

Fortunately, I was on an extremely stable footing with little debt and a healthy line of credit. Despite the lack of events to cater for, my executive leadership team stayed with me at reduced salaries (which we made up for after COVID). Many others filed for unemployment.

Thanks to PPP monies, EIDL grants, and SBA loans, we were able to prepare for the post-COVID future (hat tip to Uncle Sam). I chose to keep all my sales and marketing team members—and even added more.

Nothing lasts forever, and it was clear to me that post-pandemic there would be a rush for wedding dates. Rather than cut back on marketing, we amplified it, even creating our own YouTube channel. When couples were ready to rebook, we wanted to be their first call.

We also invested in Grant Cardone online sales training. Pre-pandemic, we catered an event for his team at a private residence. I'd never heard of Grant, but as a motivational speaker and author, he's in the same league as Tony Robbins. (I planned an event for Robbins one night at Villa Woodbine. Two hours before his arrival time, his assistant called and said they were not coming. We kept the money, and my catering team and planners pigged out on the meal, washing it down with libations that had been reserved for Tony and his team.)

Every day during the COVID shutdown, my team and I dug into the Cardone program. We also recorded our own state-of-the-art training videos that team members can view online, making them available to staffing agencies and other caterers.

We emerged from the pandemic with the best-trained catering sales team in the country—I truly believe that. And without COVID, we probably wouldn't have taken those extra steps.

If you stop growing, you begin dying. So, while other businesses were busy trying to keep their doors open, we weren't just honing our sales skills, we were expanding.

By mid-summer of 2020, the pent-up demand for weddings was mind-boggling—and we were ready. With so many outdoor venues—including my own Villa Woodbine—Florida was an especially hot market. The prime dates on our catering calendar were snatched up, and many couples opted for smaller, weeknight weddings just to secure a date. Summertime weddings in our air-conditioned tent in 2021 were triple what they normally would be.

Blue Plate Catering in Madison, Wisconsin, took the bad hand dealt by COVID and turned it into something that helped both their employees and the community. In fact, David Porto, Blue

Plate's general manager, describes the pandemic as "a turning point" for the company. He remembers the moment he realized that Blue Plate's full-time staff of 30 people could all lose their jobs due to the shutdown. "We couldn't let that happen," says David. "We have to be able to lead our team through thick *and* thin."

After all events were canceled, Blue Plate donated its perishable food to an organization serving those in need. Then David started working the phones. He knew Madison was going to be awarding contracts to caterers who could provide food to people being housed in hotels. He called the city day after day until finally Blue Plate was hired.

Blue Plate ended up serving about 400,000 individually packaged meals for breakfast, lunch, and dinner at three Madison hotels over 432 days. As part of a "Feed the Front Lines" initiative, the company also donated food and labor for thousands of meals to frontline workers at local hospitals and clinics.

As a result of the steady work, every Blue Plate employee stayed with the company throughout the pandemic, and 90 percent of them are still there. What's more, Blue Plate received the 2020 Frontline Hero Award from the National Association for Catering & Events for their dedication and charity during the COVID-19 pandemic, and for positively impacting the community. "When the going gets tough, there's always that option to say, 'Maybe it's too tough, maybe we shouldn't do it,'" says David. "But when there's a need, even if it's going to take probably a little bit more energy than what we think we can give, someone has to do it. We had to go for it."

BAILING OUT BAD SITUATIONS

Out of the corner of my eye, I saw my wife Terry jumping to safety just as the top of the event tent split open and rivers of accumulated rainwater cascaded onto six buffet lines, sending chafers, bowls, and baskets into the mud. Thirty minutes later we did something we'd never done before at an off-premise event—we evacuated the party site, leaving everything a mess. Half-eaten dinners remained on the tables overnight for the raccoons and ants to feast on.

That day in January 1995 had started out for us at 8 a.m., when our skeleton crew arrived at Birch State Park in Fort Lauderdale to cater an outdoor teambuilding event for 700 pharmaceutical firm executives. Our job was to feed them dinner at 6 p.m.

After a few innocent morning sprinkles (everyone knows that it never rains in South Florida), by early afternoon we were thankful we had brought enough rainwear for those not working underneath the tent. Speaking of the tent, the client had arranged for it. In other words, it wasn't from our usual supplier and looked suspiciously unstable. But we had other things to worry about. Besides, it never rains in South Florida.

By 2 p.m., the client was beginning to wonder if the rain would stop. Should they move dinner inside to their hotel? It wouldn't be the first time we transported our food to an indoor venue. Yet the client decided to stay at the park.

At 3 p.m., there was some light flooding. "Bill, how soon could you open the bars?" queried my client. "What time would you like them opened?" I responded. "How does 4:15 sound to you? Can you be ready by then?" the client nervously inquired. "Fine, I'll have them ready," I firmly stated.

I wondered how we could pull this one off. But why worry, we had over an hour to do the impossible.

In a few minutes, here comes the client again. "Bill, could you have the buffets ready by five rather than six?" "We'll do the best we can," I spluttered, wondering if I was truly in my right mind.

Thanks to the efforts of our staff, all eight bars and six buffets were ready on time. Ignoring the Gatorade and bottled water set out in coolers, the hungry and thirsty guests stampeded to the bars. As my five o'clock staff arrived, late from the traffic and soggy from the driving rain, the guests were sloshing through the mini marshes underneath the tent to devour our buffets of ribs, chicken, grilled mahi, seafood salad, grilled vegetables, fresh fruits, peach cobbler, and frozen yogurt. I quickly assigned each staff member a job, as the tops of my shoes were disappearing under the rapidly rising water under the tent.

The rain kept coming, and in the fading light of the afternoon we realized something had to give with the tent. The poles, which were only about two inches in diameter, were beginning to bend under the weight of the accumulating water. No one from the tent company was there to assist in bailing out the overhead ponds, so we decided to do it ourselves. But underneath one of these ponds was the power board for the 125-kilowatt generator that was supplying electricity for the tent. If we were to bail the water out, or if the tent were to split, we risked electrocuting staff and guests alike. Not a good option.

The only smart move was to cut the power before someone got hurt. As luck would have it, I was able to find the subcontractor responsible for the generator, and he turned it off. Now what? We had no electricity, it was nearly dark, there was no lighting in this part of the park, and my staff members were completely drenched. By this time most of the guests had eaten, and many were anxiously awaiting the arrival of the buses to take them back to their hotel rooms.

For some, though, the party went on. Many guests had joined us in the cook's tent, grabbing ribs and chicken from the pans meant for replenishment, and begging for more beer—which we happily supplied. Others were sliding like kids on their bellies across the rain-soaked volleyball court next to the tent.

Just then, the tent ripped open, and barrels of water crushed the buffets. My wife—who had wisely been extinguishing the Sterno flames and gathering up plates—narrowly missed being injured.

Soaked and shivering, we had to admit defeat. As the guests headed for the buses, I barked, "How many people can be here tomorrow morning at 8 a.m.?" About 15 hands went up. We returned the next morning and spent three hours cleaning up the mess as the sun shone on another beautiful South Florida day. See, it never rains in South Florida.

Sounds like a complete disaster of an event, right? Turns out, the client was delighted. We had made the party a success by opening the bars and buffets early and doing all we could to ensure the guests had a good time despite Mother Nature. The client paid in full, including the extra clean-up expenses, and tipped my team generously.

In the off-premise catering world, we are at the mercy of the weather. We can't control it, but we can plan for it. Weather plays a role in most businesses, whether big or small, impacting your clients, your products, your team, and your services.

Every business should have a plan that outlines specific steps to follow when bad weather is imminent. Share the plan with team members, secure your property, back up your online data, and establish communications procedures between you, your team, and your clients.

In tropical South Florida, we have a well-documented plan that addresses procedures and responsibilities. We review it and revise it as hurricane season is on the horizon.

Above all, be flexible. You can't control the weather, but you can control how you respond to unforeseen circumstances.

A SPOONFUL OF SUGAR HELPS THE BITTERNESS GO DOWN

When you achieve success in any type of business, you become a target for the naysayers. Criticism is a part of life. But you can choose whether to make a bitter situation worse or make it better by adding a dose of sweetness.

A few years ago, I received an email from a fellow caterer in Ohio who was offended when he saw me called a "catering guru." You see, there was a former caterer from Chicago who was known as the guru of catering—the late Mike Roman. And he deserved the title. The consummate educator collected best practices from caterers around the world, and packaged them into training seminars, conferences, books, and workshops.

In the mid-1980s, caterers like me were starving for training and education when Mike arrived to light our paths to catering success. Starting with a handful of devotees, his following grew to tens of thousands over the years, and his legend will linger for decades to come.

Here's an excerpt from the Ohio caterer's email, which was copied to some other long-time caterers in the hopes of starting a crusade of some sort:

> *While I know you have been around a long time and you have been successful in your business, I feel you are really reaching to name yourself "The Guru of Catering."*
>
> *In my opinion, Mike Roman was and always will be THE GURU OF CATERING. Yes, I would say you are an expert in our industry, but I do not see how you could claim this title ... I do find it offensive and disrespectful to Mike, and the many thousands of people in our profession that he mentored, for you to promote yourself as the guru of our industry.*

First, I did not claim to be a "guru"—someone else called me that. And for sure I don't consider myself a guru; I'm working in the trenches, not high on a mountaintop. Furthermore, I agree that Mike Roman was the one and only holder of that title.

Rather than retaliate, however, I simply extended an olive branch with a kind email, asking the caterer to join me for lunch or coffee the next time we gathered to learn from those who have followed in Mike's footsteps.

Well, we met face to face and actually hit it off. He invited me to Ohio to play a round of golf with some of the best female golfers on the LPGA Tour in a Pro Am prior to an official tournament.

Instead of making an enemy, I made a friend—and isn't that a much more enjoyable way to go through life? A couple more tips for maintaining cordial relations with competitors or others who might want to bring you down:

- Don't Take It Personally: Remember that verbal attacks are often more about the other person's insecurities or issues than they are about you. Try not to take their words to heart.
- Don't Engage: Even if you feel attacked, ask how it benefits you to respond in kind. In some cases, it may be necessary to disengage from the person, especially if they are unwilling to listen or change their behavior. Prioritize your well-being. Play the long game instead of being drawn into minor skirmishes, and look for ways to turn potential enemies into friends.

KEEP CALM AND CATER ON

It wasn't a lemon cake but a three-tier buttercream beauty adorned with fresh flowers—and it ended up bloodied and crushed on the floor of an elegant Manhattan townhouse three hours before the wedding it was made for.

On that day, David Turk—founder and president of Indiana Market & Catering in New York City—"heard the scream from hell." He was setting up for a 7 p.m. wedding on the ground floor of a four-story Fifth Avenue townhouse. Thinking someone had been shot or stabbed, he raced up the stairs to the fourth floor. There he found the venue's on-site supervisor on the ground, buttercream smearing one side of his face and blood pouring down the other, with the upside-down wedding cake next to him.

Seems the meddling manager, who wasn't involved with the wedding, had taken it upon himself to move the cake to a table he felt was a better fit (micromanagers can cause havoc, as covered in the Customer Relations chapter). While doing so, he tripped on a box the florist had left in the middle of the floor, and he and the cake came crashing down.

David sent the man to the hospital with one of his waiters and then had to figure out how to replace the cake. While the bride was in the building getting ready to say "I do," David didn't want to bother her unless absolutely necessary. Yet she had ordered the cake and hadn't given David the baker's name. "I learned that day to never cater another event without knowing the name of every vendor involved!" he says.

As luck would have it, one of his eagle-eyed waiters found the cake's receipt in a kitchen garbage bin. But the bakery was in Staten Island—which seemed so far away "it might as well have been Pennsylvania!" lamented David. When reached by phone, however, the baker laughed, which gave him hope. She said she had plenty of cakes in the freezer and she'd be able to recreate the bride's order.

The baker arrived with the new cake at 6:45, just ahead of the guests—and to this day the bride doesn't know that her original cake was replaced.

David and his team saved the day—and the bride's peace of mind—by being calm, cool, and collected. "We didn't panic, and we weren't going to stop until the problem was solved," he says. Although the mishap wasn't his fault, he found a way to fix it. Successful businesspeople like David, and the flexible baker, know how to pick up the pieces when things fall apart and deliver seamless, successful outcomes to their customers.

SOLUTIONS, SOLUTIONS, ONLY SOLUTIONS

Are you a one-man band? Do you consider your business successes to be yours and yours alone?

Most successful people don't. In an industry like catering, it takes an entire team to pull off an event. And you'll have a much easier time dealing with life's inevitable lemons if the people you surround yourself with want to pitch in and help you make the lemonade.

Chris Sanchez, managing partner of LUX Catering & Events in Salt Lake City, learned this lesson at a pivotal moment. LUX had quickly grown from a $1.5 million company to a $15 million company in less than five years. They had just started doing the kind of luxury, full-service events that would become their trademark. Thanks to their growing reputation, a well-known event planner brought LUX in to cater for a magnificent destination wedding two hours away from the city.

"We were so excited," says Chris. "It was our first time working at this ranch, which was a big deal, because at the time it was the premium destination in Utah."

It was also the first time LUX would be doing a family-style event—with food platters placed on the tables and guests serving themselves. Small problem, however: With just 30 minutes before dinner would be served, Chris discovered that not only were they missing the cake knife and server, but they had forgotten all the serving utensils for the family-style dishes. Buying more wasn't an option since the nearest store was 45 minutes away.

Devastated, Chris found the wedding planner and clued her in. "I have let you down, and I'm so sorry," he said. "I don't know how this could have happened. We checked everything a hundred times."

"It's OK," responded the unruffled planner. "Let's figure out solutions." She then suggested that dinner be served Russian-style, with staff members serving each guest at their table. They had enough utensils from the hors d'oeuvre service to make it work.

"It ended up being a huge success," says Chris. "The woman who owned the venue said it was the most beautiful service she's ever seen."

Only Chris and the planner knew about the missing serving pieces—and they remain close friends to this day. "It was such an inspiring moment to me as a young event professional," says Chris, and it influenced his own approach to leading his team when problems arise: "Let's pause before we make a decision and see if there's a solution that we can come up with together."

In Seattle, a sprinkler system caused a near disaster for Lisa Dupar Catering before the staff and rental vendor rallied together to make things right.

The catering company had set up early for a 700-person dinner auction under a tent for the Seattle Zoo. Lisa Dupar Catering had been hired for this annual event for multiple years in a row, and they had it down to a science. But for some reason, in 2022 the sprinklers went off and soaked all the tables.

When they realized what had happened, Lisa's team sprang into action. "It was just amazing how everyone kept their cool," says Lisa. Her lead server called CORT Event Rentals and requested new linens, china, and flatware. They had it all—except the flatware. So, the staff set up a sanitizing station in order to clean and dry the existing flatware.

"The team that had been working in the kitchen were about to go and take a three-hour break before coming back and working the event," says Lisa. "But instead, they said, 'No, we'll go out there and help reset.' Everybody was just unbelievable."

By working together, Lisa and her team managed to have the entire event reset and ready to go in just two hours. She says she'll never forget the words of one of her sous chefs when he heard about the dilemma. "He looked around at everybody and said, 'Only solutions, only solutions, only solutions,'" says Lisa. "Like, don't freak out, don't complain, just do it, you know? And we did. And it was amazing."

GET TO THE ROOT OF THE PROBLEM

When life gives you lemons, don't get distracted by the shiny yellow fruit. Figure out where the lemons came from, and deal with the root of the problem.

I'll never forget the way Chef Franco yelled from the passenger seat of my 1986 Ford catering van when we were towing a one-ton smoker unit mounted on a boat trailer: "Oh, no!!!" (OK, maybe those weren't his exact words, but this book is rated PG.)

On this Saturday in the mid '90s, we were on our way to Miami's Metro Zoo for a corporate barbecue. My partner, Bill, was away. It had always been his job to hook up the smoker, but this morning it fell to Franco and me.

As we rounded a curve in front of the Woman's Club of Coconut Grove and headed up a small incline, the smoker came unhitched—along with its safety chain—and barreled toward the sidewalk. Had it not been 7 a.m., people could have been seriously hurt. Thankfully, the damage was limited to two parking meters.

Everyone has had that feeling of things veering out of control. You feel lost and helpless, just like we did watching our runaway smoker. How can you turn things around?

I found great advice in a book by Shane Parrish called *Clear Thinking*. The author outlines the steps for making the best decision possible in any situation:

- Define the problem, being careful not to address the symptom, but the root problem.
- Explore possible solutions.
- Evaluate the options.
- Decide on the best option.
- Execute the best option.

Of course, this is a simplified version. But the key point is to identify the root problem and fix that problem, not the symptoms.

When we lost our smoker, the true problem we had was finding a way to cater the event while our smoker rested some 15 miles from where it should be. We could deal with the police and the trailer repair later. Since there was no way to get that trailer to the zoo, we needed to find another smoker we could use. And we did.

On another memorable day, while catering at Indian Creek Country Club, the ovens failed to ignite. Was that the problem? Not really. The problem was we needed to prepare the dinner we had been hired to serve.

Turns out a friend operated the nearby Sea View Hotel, about 15 minutes from "the Creek," as members call it. Off we went to prepare the food in the Sea View's kitchen, returning in the nick of time to delight the guests with our meal.

When dealing with adversity, don't be afraid to ask for help—as we did from our hotelier friend. You can also seek advice from colleagues in your profession. I'm a member of Certified Catering Consultants, a group of caterers from across the country who share best practices and a helping hand when needed. You'll find it easier to come back from setbacks when you're surrounded by action-oriented people who've been in your shoes rather than Debbie Downers who've thrown in the towel.

The key is to stay positive. Don't let life's lemons turn you sour. Think of all the lemonade and lemon cake you'll be rewarded with when you've overcome your difficulties.

CHAPTER 9
STAYING PROFITABLE
IT DON'T MEAN A THING IF IT DON'T GO "KA-CHING!"

HERE'S A JOKE I LIKE to tell: A man owned a small catering firm in North Dakota. The North Dakota Department of Labor claimed he was not paying proper wages to his staff and sent an agent out to interview him.

"I need a list of your employees and how much you pay them," demanded the agent.

"Well," replied the caterer, "that's easy. There's my salesperson, who's been with me for three years. I pay her $200 a week plus commission. The cook has been here for 18 months, and I pay her $300 per week.

"Then there's the half-wit who works about 18 hours every day and does about 90 percent of all the work around here. He makes about $10 per week, and I buy him a bottle of bourbon every Saturday night. He also sleeps with my wife occasionally."

"That's the guy I want to talk to," said the agent.

"That would be me," replied the caterer.

Business owners always get this joke (whether they laugh or not is another story). We've all had times when we feel we're giving everything to ensure the company's success—and not getting much in return. As I like to say, "It don't mean a thing if it don't go 'ka-ching!'" You must always remember the point of running a business—profits. If you're not making money, you're wasting your time.

FIND THOSE 10 PLACES WHERE MONEY IS HIDDEN IN YOUR BUSINESS

Former fellow professor at Florida International University Bill Quain coined the concept "10 Places Where Money Is Hidden in Your Business" and permitted me to use it. I've given many presentations to caterers based on the "10 places" principle.

The concept is to take frequent hard looks at where your money is being spent and figure out ways to save more of it. It goes hand in hand with raising revenue in any business.

Here are the top 10 places where I've found money hiding in my business. Go hunting in your own business and see what you can find.

#10 On your shelves
You must find that perfect balance between having things on hand when you need them and not overbuying. You're flushing money down the drain when inventory sits on your shelf with no ROI. And when product just sits there, it can grow legs and go out the door with an unscrupulous employee, hidden in bags, purses, and even garbage cans, to be retrieved after closing time. Cash in the bank is much more useful than cash used to overstock your inventories.

#9 In your accounts receivable
I've learned this the hard way: "Before the party, the caterer is in charge, but after the party, the client is in charge." A small hiccup in catering services can cause a client to refuse to pay the balance due. Time spent chasing down delinquents could be much better invested in generating new business.

#8 In your accounts payable
Pay bills on their due dates—unless there's a discount for early payment. Keep your money in your bank account for as long as possible.

#7 In advance deposits
In Miami, my summer monthly revenues can be as little as 10 percent of monthly revenues during high season, while overhead

expenses remain the same. Collecting advance deposits during the slower months helps keep the cash flowing.

#6 In credit card processing fees
It pays to get competitive bids on your credit card processing and to pass the charges on to your clients. My company adds 5 percent onto payments made with a credit card; we advise our customers about the charge upfront, of course.

#5 In your bank accounts
Idle cash should be earning some form of interest. I recently invested in bond funds, which pay more than money markets and are liquid. Talk to your financial advisor to learn about other ways of keeping your money working for you.

#4 In poor negotiations
Some 20 years ago I attended a weekend seminar on how to negotiate better with clients and vendors—and I've never forgotten those lessons. Listen more and talk less when negotiating. And don't be afraid to ask, "Can you do better?" Usually, they can—and they will.

#3 In your failure to upsell
A few years ago, a client on Key Biscayne said he had to talk to me personally before his daughter's Vizcaya wedding. When my event producer and I arrived at his multimillion-dollar home on the water, we found him armed with an Excel spreadsheet. *Get ready for some negotiations!* I thought.

Turns out, the father was concerned about the level of service, knowing that Vizcaya is a tough place to work. All he wanted was extra servers, and he was willing to pay for them. An easy fix—and one we could have easily upsold without being prompted. Consider all the extras your clients would pay more for *and offer them.* We've learned that most clients will pay a minimum of 20 percent more than the quoted price on the original proposal for extra services and items.

#2 In your payroll expenses

It's easy for business owners hellbent on good service to let payroll costs skyrocket—and then realize that there's no money left for them. Keep an eagle eye on this expense, making sure your pricing factors in your payroll expenses.

#1 In lazy purchasing

Put in place purchasing procedures to ensure you're not losing money out the back door. Lazy people don't bother to look on the shelves or in the refrigerators before buying food items. Lazy people don't get competitive bids. Lazy people don't take the time to negotiate purchase prices. And lazy people will not be working for me for very long.

FOLLOW THE LEAD OF SUCCESSFUL COMPETITORS

If you're struggling to stay profitable, you're not alone. According to the U.S. Bureau of Labor Statistics, 65 percent of businesses fail during their first 10 years. In fact, only 25 percent make it to the 15-year mark.

What are the secrets of those companies that make it? If you're smart, you'll find out. Look to others in your same line of business, and try to learn what they do—and what they don't do.

A great way to accomplish this is by joining a professional organization. I'm a member of a group that I founded—the Leading Caterers of America (LCA), a consortium of top caterers from the U.S. and Canada. I've gotten to know fellow colleagues very well in this group, and we often share best practices. Through LCA and other professional organizations, I've met and learned lessons from fellow entrepreneurs from across the country.

One impressive caterer I've gotten to know through LCA is Jesse Bullard, vice president of Southern Way Catering in Columbia, South Carolina. He shared one of the most important lessons he's learned from his business partner Jimmy Stevenson, who founded Southern Way: "The difference between a good caterer and a great caterer is their ability to anticipate problems and solve them before they happen."

This key lesson was put to the test early in Jesse's career when he agreed to help another caterer feed the media crews at the 2012 Democratic National Convention in Charlotte, North Carolina.

Not knowing what to expect, Jesse and his team found themselves catering around the clock. With only two hours to sleep each night, Jesse made his bed out of broken-down boxes on the floor of the kitchen trailer. The team faced incredibly stringent food-handling rules, last-minute requests from the media for coffee service at 4 a.m., and even a tent that caught on fire (quickly put out with a fire extinguisher, thankfully). "We weren't prepared to function at that level," admits Jesse.

But they learned a valuable lesson from the ordeal: "On those larger events, you really have to add a lot of cushion to make it make sense." In other words, factor in the extra time needed for staff members to perform their jobs well—and charge accordingly. When we interviewed Jesse in April 2024, his team had just returned from flawlessly catering a large PGA Tour event in Hilton Head for tens of thousands of golfers, sponsors, and guests. Lessons like the ones learned in Charlotte prepared the Southern Way team for Hilton Head and other large events they service each year.

Stories like Jesse's inspire me to do better. If your business is ailing and you can't figure out why, seek out colleagues whose businesses you admire. More often than not, you'll find them to be helpful and willing to share their experiences. And their advice may open your eyes to problems in your business that you've failed to notice previously.

KEEP YOUR ACCOUNTS RECEIVABLE CURRENT

I often tell my team, "We are not a bank!" If clients need a loan to pay us, they should go to their bank for a loan or use a credit card. I want my accounts receivable to be at a rock-bottom minimum.

There are myriad ways to keep your accounts receivable current. Here are some tips:

- Offer discounts for early payment, such as a 2 percent discount if paid within 10 days.
- Make sure payment terms are clearly documented on your invoices and statements, including due dates and penalties for late payments.
- Use a software program that automatically generates invoices, statements, and reminders for payment due dates. Invoicing errors can lead to disputes and slow collections, so issuing the correct invoice is important.
- Consider requiring credit checks to eliminate clients who won't be able to pay their bills. You could also place spending limits on certain clients, depending on the results of a credit check.
- Implement late-payment fees.

Collection agencies and legal action should be the last resort, because then you're spending money to get your money.

For clients who simply can't pay the entire invoice, work something out. Recently, I suffered a business financial loss from a bad investment, which resulted in me being liable for a significant amount of money—in the low six figures. I worked out a financing plan to pay every expense over time, which preserved my cash flow. Remember—cash is king!

DON'T UNDERESTIMATE THE IMPORTANCE OF STRONG VENDOR RELATIONSHIPS

A friend in South Florida—let's call him John—started a small business in 2005 that grew to be successful. One of the keys to John's prosperity is his remarkable ability to manage his accounts payable.

You see, John understands the importance of strong vendor relationships. He stays in close contact with his suppliers. By forging these ties, he's able to negotiate favorable terms for his business. He's built up trust with these vendors, who sometimes allow him to extend his payment terms when necessary.

That's an important advantage in a place like South Florida, where the weather can influence cash flow. Basically, John's business has eight good months—during the fall, winter, and spring seasons—but in the summer, business dries up. He's able to manage payments successfully during the slower season by projecting cash flow and negotiating strong vendor discounts.

In my business, revenue drops tenfold during the summer months, yet there are still bills to pay. To help address the problem, we set up an advance deposit system for our clients who have booked events at Villa Woodbine during the busier season. In fact, we will offer small upgrades—such as a complimentary welcome drink or ice cream with the wedding cake—to encourage customers to pay larger advance deposits.

The deposits, which are due during the months we need it most (June through September), help us to stay current on our bills over the slow season, and we invest the excess in money market funds to earn interest.

We also rank our accounts payable. First comes payroll, since neglecting to pay employees on time will implode a business. Rent, utilities, and sales tax are the next most important payments. Other expenses come next, and careful negotiations with vendors means we often have flexibility when we need it. Since we pay bills on time during peak season, vendors often work with us to extend payment terms during slow season. This system has worked well over five decades, as my team and I have maintained a stellar reputation while staying in the black since 1980.

I've struggled at times with insufficient cash to pay bills when they are due—and I'm sure I'm not the only one. When this occurs, I call my vendor/creditor, explain my situation, and work out ways to pay over time—preferably without any interest or late fees. When you're a good customer with a long track record of on-time payments, suppliers will generally offer you better terms.

Here's a key strategy that I learned long ago: First you negotiate the price, then you negotiate the terms. Smart vendors who are financially stable will accommodate interest-free payment terms to keep the business of a valued customer.

Your reputation matters, and owing vendors without a discussion can ruin any business. Bottom-line advice: Stay current on your payables because you will get better vendor pricing than those who are past due. Vendors raise prices for slow payers. And on those rare occasions when you need more time to pay, a good track record means vendors are much more likely to work with you.

SEEK FEEDBACK TO AVOID POTENTIAL PROBLEMS THAT COULD DRAG DOWN PROFITS

Never underestimate the importance of feedback from clients as well as teammates. I send out an online feedback form to each customer, offering a small reward—such as an Amazon gift card—if they complete it. In this way, we constantly monitor our performance—and nip small problems in the bud before they become a drag on profits.

On a scale of 1 to 5, we average about 4.7. We're not perfect, and there are always things to improve upon. In addition to space where the customer can write comments, the form includes the following questions, which can be modified to use in any business:

- Which event producer did you work with?
- How satisfied were you with the preparation, assistance, and helpfulness prior to the event?
- How satisfied were you with the friendliness and professionalism of the on-site day-of staff?
- How satisfied were you with the taste of the food?
- How satisfied were you with the presentation of the menu items?
- How satisfied were you with the quality of beverages?

- How satisfied were you with the comfort of the venue?
- How satisfied were you with the overall value spent on catering?
- How satisfied were you with the overall experience?
- How likely are you to refer a client to us?

In years past, several customers complained about our tequila policy. We had banned tequila from being served at our events because guests tended to abuse it, and then our staff had to clean up unpleasant messes. We listened to the complaints, however, and amended the policy. Now we do serve tequila, but it must be served with a mixer—no shots allowed.

As I write this, I'm looking at a review from an event we catered at the Bonnet House, a historic home in Fort Lauderdale. We received all 5s except for one 4, which had to do with the customer's perception of the value they received for what they spent on catering. We followed up—*always follow up!*—and it turns out our price was much higher than the two other caterers who bid on their wedding.

While the clients had hoped for a lower bill, they were ecstatic about what we delivered. Regarding our event producer Gipsy Williams and our event manager Isabelle Blouin, they wrote:

> *Gipsy and Isabelle were hands-down amazing! Gipsy was extremely easy to work with and very kind.* [We stress treating people with love and kindness during our training.] *Isabelle made sure we were comfortable the whole time during the wedding. Their attention to detail and attentiveness was beyond our expectations. The ladies and their team made our experience with Bill Hansen unforgettable. Our guests continue to tell us the food was the best they ever had at a wedding. And the servers and bartenders were excellent.*

When you get customer feedback, not only should you follow up with the client, you should share it with all departments involved—especially the sales team. Since your sales team is the first point of contact, doesn't it make sense to give them client feedback to help them grow in their roles?

There's another group that salespeople should hear feedback from—the team that delivers the sale. In their quest to seal the deal, salespeople sometimes overpromise. That puts excess stress on the operations and culinary teams.

To prevent that problem, at my company we have the culinary and ops teams write up a post-event review, which is then shared with the sales team. I remind my team frequently to only sell events that the culinary and operations teams can deliver. And if there are issues with the event due to miscalculations by the sales team, we need to fix them.

MAKE YOUR CASH WORK FOR YOU

If you don't invest your idle cash, you're leaving money on the table.

At my company, we invest funds that are not currently needed—such as advance deposits—into a money market account, earning daily interest. You could also work with a financial firm and invest idle cash in stocks, bonds, gold, or REITs.

And here's a tip—rather than selling your investment assets when you need cash, consider pledging them to a bank to obtain a revolving line of credit, which is a credit line that remains available even as you pay the balance. In the past, I've pledged a certain portion of my portfolio to my bank as security in case of default. The best part is that a line of credit is different than a loan, in that you only use it when needed, and can pay it back as needed. Assuming the market is rising, you'll continue to increase your wealth while using the line of credit during slow seasons, paying it down during busy times of the year. Keep in mind that if your investments lose value, the bank will lower the amount of your credit line.

Investing extra cash in something that will benefit your business is another great use of funds. For example, in the mid-teens we bought our own 8,000-square-foot commissary in Opa-locka, where prices were low. We paid cash for the building—a former airplane landing gear repair facility—and retrofitted it into exactly what we needed. It's located only 20 to 25 minutes from the heart of Miami.

Even when you're not flush, keep your eyes peeled for investments that will pay off in the future. I learned this the hard way in 1988, when I had the opportunity to buy Villa Woodbine since my lease gave me first right of refusal. I didn't have the money for the purchase so passed on the opportunity. Now, however, I wish I had found an investment partner—the property has increased tenfold in value, and it continues to be the cornerstone of my business, providing nearly half of our revenue. Rent for the villa has skyrocketed. Owning is far superior to renting in nearly every business, as you build equity and have more control over your day-to-day operations.

NEGOTIATE WELL NOW, SAVE MONEY LATER

Negotiations done right can save significant amounts of money when dealing with clients as well as vendors.

One of the most important lessons I've learned in my career is to always ask one simple question: "Can you do better?" When reviewing quotes for products and services, for example, I always ask this question—and frequently end up with a better price. I recently asked a sound engineer this question and saved 20 percent. If you start doing the same, you'll be amazed at the results—and you'll cover the cost of this book times a thousand.

Asking the "can you do better" question was a tip I picked up from a negotiating class I took. One day, the instructor gave each student a bit of homework—to return to class with a story about how they negotiated with a vendor for a lower price. One young lady surprised us all by recounting how she negotiated with a toll booth attendant to allow her to exit the Florida Turnpike for free. It took her a few minutes to make the deal, but she did it by crafty negotiating and a long face.

To make all your deals sweeter, remember these tips:

1. **Negotiations can't begin until you know your true costs.** How can you set yourself up to be profitable when you don't know the worth of what you're selling? You must walk into any negotiation knowing the floor of what you'll accept—and that requires research ahead of time. For example, when I'm negotiating for catering, I know the per-person minimum it takes for my company to profit from an event. If I'm talking to a lowballing couple about their wedding and they won't agree to that minimum, I'll walk away, telling them they're better off with a less expensive caterer. And I'll often refer them to one.
2. **Relationships matter.** We've had a great relationship with our rental equipment supplier since 1988. Not only does the company offer amazing service and meaningful discounts, it has comped many of our fundraising events for charity and company parties. As a result of the mutual trust we've built up over the years, we just negotiated a 2 percent rebate with this vendor—which adds up to more than $20,000 per year.
3. **Reputations matter.** Clients will often agree to a higher price when you share your accolades. For example, we always make sure potential clients know that we are a member of Leading Caterers of America, that we were voted by Miami residents as the best catering and wedding venue in Miami, and that we've catered for four U.S. presidents and Pope John Paul II. This way, no one can question our credentials—and some clients like to brag about the background of their caterer.
4. **Listening matters.** Remember, everyone has two ears and one mouth for a reason. Repeat clients' must-haves back to them so they know you understand and will give them what they need, not what you want. This brings clients closer to closing the sale.

5. **Know your limits.** Let's face it—some things are non-negotiable. But you need to know what they are before going into any negotiation. For example, when we negotiate a catering contract, we have wiggle room on the menu items. Clients can choose chicken instead of steak, for example, to bring costs down. However, I will never compromise on the number of staff it takes to cater an event. If we remove staff, service will be sacrificed, and both the event and our reputation will suffer.
6. **Don't undercut yourself.** The best negotiators never say, "Let's split the difference." It's better to gradually reduce the price and retain more of your profits. Let's say a client wishes to reduce the cost by $10 per person. If we "split the difference," we would be offering a $5 discount per person. Rather, after making some alterations to what will be provided, we will counter with a price reduction of $1 or $2 per person.
7. **Preserve your cash flow.** If you can't negotiate a lower price, it can pay off to negotiate when a payment is due. For example, my landlord at Villa Woodbine once asked for a rent increase from $8,000 to $10,000 per month for a five-year lease. I proposed averaging out the increase by paying $8,000 in year one, $9,000 in year two, $10,000 in year three, $11,000 in year four, and $12,000 in year five. My landlord still received his rent of $10,000/month, but it was backloaded to protect our cash flow as well as counter inflation.
8. **Ask for early-payment discounts.** On the other hand, some vendors offer an early-payment discount, such as 2/10 net 30—if you pay the invoice within 10 days, you'll receive a 2 percent discount. Otherwise, the full amount is due within 30 days. Have you ever thought about approaching a vendor and asking for 3/10 net 30? This can work. Remember, always ask, "Can you do better?"

9. **Plan ahead.** In the heat of the moment, we sometimes pay more than we should because we did not plan appropriately. For example, the price of whole beef tenderloin increases in December, as demand rises—and at my company, we serve tons of beef tenderloin during the holidays. So we negotiate for a certain price in October and then take delivery as needed. Huge savings.

SOMETIMES YOU HAVE TO SPEND TO SAVE

When you're negotiating, there can be a tendency to think, "Everything's on the table!" But is it really? If you undercut your most important assets, you'll lose money in the long run.

In my line of work, payroll is by far the largest expense. It takes an army to serve even 100 guests at an off-premise event. As many as 20 team members are on-site—and that's not counting the admin work beforehand, the warehouse work, the sales work, and the food prep prior to the event. One of the easiest ways to lower the price of an event would be to cut the number of staff working.

But we don't. We know that our reputation hinges on the level of service clients and their guests experience. In fact, we pay more to hire top-notch servers. If your standard for filling a position is a warm body, you'll provide lukewarm service—or worse.

We rely exclusively on our A team members during the off-season and shoulder season. During peak season, when there's not enough talent to go around, we supplement the ranks with B and C team members. And we charge more to offset the extra expense.

That's the key: Whatever your "non-negotiable" is, account for its cost in your pricing.

CHAPTER 10
LEADERSHIP
GO BIG OR GO HOME

LEADERSHIP IS NOT ABOUT BEING perfect but about continually striving to improve.

In my early years, I led by giving orders. That can work in the short term. But to get long-term, repeatable results from your team, you need a more collaborative approach. Team members must understand and buy into your vision. And no one's buying into a guy barking demands without rhyme or reason.

I like to consider this leadership question: "Am I a thermostat or a thermometer?" Am I setting the tone for my team and leading us by example to greater heights? Or am I reacting to every inevitable business setback and success, wavering up and down depending on the day, and projecting volatility? Be strong. Be steady. And be an inspirational leader that your team can emulate.

LEADERS MAKE TIMELY DECISIONS

Ready, fire, aim.

I have been guilty of this many times in my career.

Fortunately, in my fourth quarter century on earth, I have learned to do more due diligence and listen to all sides of the issue before pulling the trigger.

It is not always easy. Paralysis by analysis is foreign to me. And the greater the risk, the greater the reward.

Leadership in any business involves daily decision-making that impacts the lives of others—your team, your clients, and your community. No leader bats 100 percent, but here are the steps I follow:

- Gather the facts, leaving out the drama.
- Ask questions to clarify the facts.
- Gain wise counsel from others.
- Then pull the trigger, informing everyone of your decision and why you made it, and asking them for their support.

There is a fine balance between rushed decisions and those that drag out way too long. Some of my best hiring decisions have been made on the spot, while some of my worst happened by default because I waited too long to decide.

In late August 2017, we had less than 24 hours to prepare 3,000 meals for Hurricane Irma victims evacuated from the Florida Keys—a job we repeated for 10 days. There was no time to "think about it." If we waited, we would lose the business and those evacuees would not be fed as quickly. I made the decision to accept the challenge, and by six the following morning we were on-site at the Miami-Dade Fairgrounds.

Of course, there were hiccups along the way, but I will never forget the smiles on the faces of those stranded when they tasted their first hot meal in days. This is why we do what we do.

On another memorable day—December 30, 2013—I received a frantic call from an event planner who needed our help. Could we prepare food for 250 guests and have it ready in 30 hours, along with service staff, bartenders, tables, chairs, linens, china, flatware, and stemware?

Seems that a Star Island celeb had invited some 250 or so of his friends and wannabe friends for dinner at his mansion overlooking the Miami lights along Biscayne Boulevard, to be followed by an all-night party for 1,800 or more. Originally, the in-house chef was going to cook for everyone, but as the guest list ballooned into triple digits, he cried, "Help!"

To make matters more complicated, staff members would need to be bused from Watson Island to Star Island, a mile or so away, due to stringent security and lack of parking.

I made a few phone calls to see if we could pull off this daunting task and then pulled the trigger: Yes, we were in.

Staffing was no problem. The lure of double pay and the star-studded guest list had staff calling us for work that night, canceling their own plans for a New Year's Eve to remember.

Meanwhile, in our commissary, our chefs called our loyal suppliers for urgent deliveries that needed to arrive that day or at sunrise the following morning. Fortunately, we pay our bills on time and have been customers for decades, so they were happy to accommodate.

The client had his own vodka brand and was going to provide all the alcohol, but we needed to provide the glassware, mixers, ice, and—of course—first-class bartenders.

After working feverishly into the night, with early wakeups for my culinary team on New Year's Eve, the food was ready on time. Carved beef tenderloins; a raw bar overflowing with stone crabs, jumbo shrimp, ceviche, clams, and oysters; freshly made pasta; sushi; and sweets galore were delivered to the makeshift kitchen in the celeb's multiple-car garage and cooked to order on-site.

The party lasted until daybreak on New Year's Day, and my team spent most of the holiday in bed, recovering from a night to remember for a lifetime. We had pulled off the glitzy gala for Sean Combs, aka P. Diddy, and his celebrity guest list, which included Jay-Z, Beyoncé, and scores of big names in entertainment and sports.

If I had hesitated, or doubted our ability, we would have left a lot of money on the table—not to mention stories of a quintessential Miami New Year's Eve bash.

Failure to make timely decisions can be horrible for morale. People love managers who don't keep them hanging—who decide *and*, if they make a mistake, own up to it, fix it, and move on.

When it comes to operational decision-making—such as where to buy, who to hire, what to serve, and when to close a date because we are booked to capacity—those decisions are made by my department heads, who are given parameters, since they are working *in* the business, while I work *on* the business.

And their compensation depends upon how well they make those decisions. A good leader makes timely decisions and knows which decisions to trust in the hands of others.

LEADERS PROVIDE STRUCTURE

Art Fortuna, a foodservice veteran based in Portland, Oregon, was hired as a consultant for a catering firm that had landed the foodservice contract for the Portland Art Museum, taking the firm's annual revenues from $400,000 to $3.5 million pretty much overnight.

A great windfall for a small company, right? It should have been. But the firm was hemorrhaging money. "They were struggling with how to manage it all," explains Art.

When Art arrived, he found a group of enthusiastic, talented people who wanted to create a quality product for their customers. But staff meetings were chaotic. Everyone chimed in with ideas, but no one took charge and turned those ideas into realities. Art had to focus the team.

"The phenomenon of management is a series of decisions," he says. "The worst decision is no decision. I'd let everyone have their say and then say, 'OK, this is what we're going to do.' It's deciding, coming up with a plan, letting everybody know about the plan, and then moving forward. Afterward you follow up and ask, 'How did we do?'"

The buck stopped with Art—and employees appreciated that someone had filled the leadership vacuum. "Many came up to me to say how much they appreciated me being there and being a steady hand," he says. "It took the pressure off them."

Of course, exerting power will always ruffle some feathers. To keep things running smoothly, Art follows what he calls a "reasonable man approach." He tries to learn as much as possible about an issue before making a reasonable decision, which he can then rationalize to any team member who might question it. While making changes at the company, Art emphasized that he would bear the consequences if things went south. After hearing the reasoning, if someone still didn't want to fulfill their role, he let them know they might be a better fit somewhere else.

His strategies worked. In the years he's been with the company, Art—now senior partner—has quadrupled revenues to eight figures. He's now working less *in* the business and more *on* the business, after putting in place a formidable team of managers who report to him.

Recently, Art brought an executive on board to be the conduit of communication between him and the team. The new hire has implemented the RAPID decision-making process, which was originally created by consulting firm Bain & Company. With RAPID, team members are assigned to five key roles: Recommend, Agree, Perform, Input, and Decide. The structure is freeing for people, says Art, as it clearly defines each person's responsibilities: "They can do what they need to do and not have to worry about being second-guessed. And that's a great way to lead people."

LEADERS DELEGATE

A decade ago, I was standing next to another owner of a catering firm by a sink in a Vegas restroom at a catering conference. He was talking to an employee on his cell phone, telling him where to set the coffee urn at a client's office. The other caterer had been in business longer than me but hadn't yet figured out how to delegate the minor decisions so that he could work on the major ones.

For the first 20 years of my catering business, I micromanaged every decision and every event, down to calculating how many scoops of ice cream would come from a three-gallon container.

Slowly, I gave the reins to others, providing them with the tools and training to do their jobs effectively. To say this was easy would be a lie. I agonized about whether the guests would be delighted if I wasn't orchestrating everything. Guess what—they were! And I found that many of my managers did things better than me.

My company now caters for as many as seven major events concurrently across South Florida on a busy Saturday night. That wouldn't be possible if I still held onto the reins as tightly as I once had. Slowly delegating tasks and duties to others will help your business grow to the next level.

When I delegate, I clearly define tasks and expectations. Each executive, for example, is responsible for key performance indicators, which include sales growth, labor cost, cost of sales, and gross margins. The goals are clear but also challenge them to do better.

You must know your team well enough to delegate based on each person's strengths and skills. Good leaders see beyond what team members do; they envision what each team member *could* do. With our service team, for example, we give top servers the opportunity to be assistant event managers, working under the direction of event managers. As they grow and learn, they can become event managers themselves one day.

I've watched in amazement as team members over the years have grown from entry-level employees to managers. A woman who started doing culinary prep work, for example, took over our school catering operation for two years after the Great Recession—and she rocked it. By providing opportunities for team members to grow and advance, we reduce turnover and help our valued employees thrive and prosper.

LEADERS MANAGE PRIORITIES

We've all been guilty of allowing the urgent to take precedence over the important.

Authoring this book was important—but not urgent. Dealing with leads, clients, and staff is usually important and urgent, but in most cases, responses can wait until working hours.

While being available for customer service, I have learned to carve out time to accomplish what Jim Collins and Jerry Porras call "BHAGs"—Big Hairy Audacious Goals—in their book *Built to Last: Successful Habits of Visionary Companies.*

Are you sacrificing your long-term goals while running the daily rat race? If your answer is "yes," you need a time-management plan.

We all need quiet time to work on the big-picture projects. And many businesspeople kick them down the road and think, "Someday I'll do it." But that "someday" never comes as we simply keep on keeping on.

I manage my time by rising early for prayer and meditation before delving into my plans for the day. I have learned that the more time I spend quietly sitting with the Lord, and listening to his voice, the better prepared I am to tackle the day, rather than be tackled by it.

During this time, I keep a pad next to me in my office easy chair and scribble follow-up notes from the day before and new to-dos for the day. Next, I enter these tasks in Microsoft To Do, look at what I did not finish the day before, and plan my day rather than let my day plan me.

And not until then do I look at my email. Email is what others want us to do. Yes, that is important, but not until we have planned what we must do.

By the time I arrive at my business, I have completed those tasks that I can do without the help of others. First thing upon arrival, I walk through my offices, commissary, and warehouse and say "good morning" to my team. Although I have meetings scheduled on most days, I still leave plenty of time to deal with the unexpected.

One wonderful planning tool I recommend is the Eisenhower Matrix, also known as the Urgent-Important Matrix, which helps prioritize tasks. It was developed by Stephen Covey, who based it on a quote by President Dwight D. Eisenhower: "I have two kinds of problems, the urgent and the important. The urgent are not important, and the important are never urgent."

The matrix is divided into four quadrants, with the first quadrant representing tasks that are important and urgent, and the fourth quadrant representing tasks that are not important and not urgent. Give it a try and see if it helps you better focus on your long-term goals.

One thing is certain: Time is finite. Learn to live every day like it is your last. And if you can spend money to save time, giving you more bandwidth to focus on what's important, do it! You can't take it with you.

LEADERS COMMUNICATE CLEARLY AND ACTIVELY LISTEN

Leaders who communicate well are hard to find. But my friend Jim Horan, CEO of Blue Plate Catering in Chicago, mastered the skill early on, and it's helped him become one of the top caterers in the country.

"As a former social worker, I learned to be a good listener and the right questions to ask," explains Jim. In fact, Jim believes that being a good listener is the most important skill a person can have when it comes to both employee and customer relations.

"When you listen to people, you help them solve their problems," he says. "People are going to tell you what they need."

Jim's catering career started in the early 1980s when he delivered meals to film crews. He then opened Blue Plate Deli across the street from Wrigley Field, coming up with the memorable slogan "Blue Plate: Only 200 Yards from Home Plate."

Starting as a one-man band, Jim now conducts a symphony orchestra of over 1,000 team members. Blue Plate Catering is expected to achieve between $45 million and $50 million in revenue in 2024.

The company's mantra is "care more," reflecting Jim's belief that all businesses are in the people business. He encourages team members to express their ideas and concerns, and empowers them to make decisions. By prioritizing communication, Jim continues to lead the company to even greater success.

Strong leaders must also communicate well with customers. When event planner Gladys Mezrahi first takes on a client, for example, she continually asks questions until she gets to the heart of the company's goals. "Every single event has a different objective," says Gladys. "That's where I come in, narrowing down on what they really want and what they really need."

One company hired Gladys to create a ribbon-cutting event for a new building. No problem, said Gladys, but what do you want the "takeaway" to be for attendees? The underlying goal, the client divulged, was to get people interested in the development's second tower, which wasn't yet under construction.

Armed with that feedback, Gladys hired a sand-sculpture artist to be on location at the event, building a replica of the second tower out of sand. Guests loved seeing the artist in action, snapping photos, sharing them to social media, and generating a buzz that reached far beyond the one-day event. By asking questions of her client and listening to the answers, Gladys was able to lead them to a solution that accomplished their goal.

If you plan what you're going to say next while the other person is still talking, stop. Actively listen. As I tell my sales team, the best way to sell is to ask questions.

And the same holds true for leaders. Do you ask your team questions before deciding on an issue? And do you repeat back your understanding of what they said? That's a good trick for communicating well—sometimes what you say is not what they hear, and vice versa. Get your team's input and make sure you understand it.

LEADERS SHOW EMPATHY

Three generations of Bonuras have made Bonura Hospitality Group in upstate New York a success story since its founding in 1971. One reason for its longevity is the family atmosphere that extends to all staff and customers.

"It's a family business, and we try to treat everyone like family," says Mike Bonura, principal.

For example, Mike has made it a point to learn some Spanish so he can make his Latino team members feel more comfortable. "I always try to communicate in my broken Spanish, because I want them to understand that I care," he says. "There's an added level of respect because they can see that I'm trying."

Mike considers mutual respect to be the most important trait in a leader. "Never feel that you are better than anyone who's working for you, no matter the role—the porter that unloads the truck, the person that scrubs the toilet, or your executive chef or business partner," he stresses. "The only thing that I know after a lot of years in this business is that I don't know it all."

The Bonura approach to leadership has engendered loyalty among staff members, many of whom have been with the company for decades.

Every human being on Planet Earth wants to feel secure, significant, and accepted. As I walk through my venues and kitchens, I try to ask my team members, "What can I do for you?" Normally, they say, "Bill, everything is good. Thank you for asking."

But sometimes I get the privilege of serving them.

One day as I arrived at work, one of my warehouse workers was standing outside, animatedly speaking on his phone. I could see he was upset.

Keep in mind this is a young man who lives in the inner city who'd already been through many struggles in his life. He had bounced from job to job, but he found a home with us.

"Alan," I asked, "what is going on? Can you share with me?" He opened up, telling me that his income tax return money had been stolen through identity fraud, and he needed $400 for a small scooter to drive to work. We lent him the money he needed with a minor weekly paycheck deduction until he received his stolen money from the IRS. Alan paid back the loan and, as I write this, is now in his third year with my company.

I've made my living in the hospitality business. We can't provide kind, hospitable service to our external customers unless we model it to our internal customers. Lead from the heart.

LEADERS DREAM BIG ... AND THEN GO FOR IT

"If you don't know where you're going, you might wind up someplace else." That quote is attributed to Yogi Berra, the great Yankee catcher, who was known for pithy sayings that sometimes didn't make sense. You get where he's coming from, though—to get where you want to be, you need a plan.

Here's another quote that rings true: "Failing to plan is planning to fail."

When we plan, we risk failure. But there's no risk in planning if you fail to act. That's why many business leaders never get from point A to point B—they're afraid of what might happen. They are afraid of failure.

If you visualize something with passion and belief, and you embark on a journey toward that goal, your chances of achieving it are much greater than if you simply go through the motions with no belief, passion, determination, conviction, or enthusiasm.

Some 45 years ago, I traveled down South Bayshore Drive in Coconut Grove, admiring the mansions lining the drive, some overlooking the bay. I pledged to myself that one day I'd live there. Six years later, I moved into one of those mansions, Villa Woodbine, which is still my business's stronghold, though I don't live there anymore.

As I write this, I'm visualizing myself shooting my age in golf, traveling to Israel (once there is peace) and hanging out on the hill where Jesus delivered his Sermon on the Mount, but most of all sharing my love and kindness with those in my employ, those I meet, and my clients—many of whom have been with me for decades. I can see it, and I know in my soul I'll get there.

What lights your fire? What have you wanted to do in business but never took the time to pursue? Is now the time to get started?

Ask yourself: Is my goal specific? Is it measurable? Is it attainable? Is it realistic? And what's my timetable for reaching it?

Think big! Forget about those imaginary boxes that everyone says you must stay inside. There's a world out there that needs you. The Lord gave you gifts! Don't disappoint him by not putting them to good use.

Most people my age will tell you this: Life flies by faster every year. It's hard to grasp this when you're young, but time is short. Set your sights on something bigger than yourself. Aim high and get to work.

The ball is in your court. Take these inspirational stories and run with them. I live my life by this motto: "You're never too old, and it's never too late to turn your dreams into reality."

ACKNOWLEDGMENTS

For their contributions to this book, the co-authors wish to thank:

- Jesse Bullard, vice president of Southern Way Catering Inc. in South Carolina, who shared such stories as how he outfoxed an unreasonable vendor.
- Michael "Funky" Forgus, owner of Cincinnati's leading caterer, DelightMore, who shared how he merged two catering brands into one.
- Art Fortuna, president and CEO of VT Group, who began his career in corporate foodservice, and transferred his talents to salvage a struggling catering firm in Portland, turning it into Oregon's leading caterer.
- Chuck Mercurio, the consummate restaurant executive, who took dining in Miami to new heights in the late 20th century. He could write his own book but has shared some stories with us.
- Jeffrey Miller, CEO of Jeffrey A. Miller Catering in Philadelphia, whose friendship over the years has led to sales growth in Bill Hansen Catering through his company Party Space. He has taken venue relations to a whole new level in Philadelphia, as the city's Leading Caterer of America.
- Dewey LoSasso, Bill Hansen's corporate executive chef, who has led the culinary team to new heights.
- Elizabeth Silverman, whose Lovables Catering & Kitchen brand has expanded Hansen Group's borders into corporate budget-conscious catering.

- Lisa Dupar, owner of Lisa Dupar Catering in Redmond, Washington, who shared educational and inspirational stories.
- Executive recruiter David Kohlasch of Patrice & Associates.
- Anthony Lambatos, CEO of Footers Catering in Arvada, Colorado, who inspires business leaders to MIBE (Make It Better Everyday) with his keynote addresses and training programs.
- Michael Bonura, partner at Bonura Hospitality, who inspired Bill Hansen Catering to innovate with group tastings, which have worked perfectly.
- David Porto, general manager of Blue Plate Catering in Madison, Wisconsin, who is gaining an amazing reputation in his market.
- Gladys Mezrahi, president and CEO of Miami's Indigo Events, whose unique approach to event planning puts her at the top of the international event planning world.
- Jim Horan, CEO of Blue Plate Catering in Chicago, a former social worker who catapulted from food deliveries to heading one of the city's top catering brands.
- John Bach, executive chef and founder of Seoul Food Korean BBQ in Los Angeles, who shared how he focuses on the guest experience.
- Chris Sanchez, managing partner of LUX Catering & Events in Salt Lake City, whose enthusiastic and creative approach to not only catering but unique designs and florals makes him one of Utah's most sought-after caterers.
- Meryl Snow, Bill's friend for decades, who is co-founder of Feastivities Events in Philadelphia and principal consultant of SnowStorm Solutions.
- Sean Sweeney, account executive at CP Communications.
- David Turk, consultant at David Turk Consulting and president of Indiana Market & Catering, who shared a compelling story of how to deal with adversity under intense pressure.

- Tracy Vessillo, president of Florida's Puff 'n Stuff Catering, formerly president of Wolfgang Puck Catering, who shared stories stressing the importance of quality and culture.
- Chris Villard, who has rocked the catering scene in Georgia.
- Rachael Volz, CEO and owner of Houston's A Fare Extraordinaire and The Revaire, whose exacting operational standards are an inspiration to many.
- Joseph Venemen, founder and CEO of StaffMate Online, who was first to develop and market online software for scheduling staff.

Bill Hansen wishes to thank:

- Sara Perez Webber, my esteemed co-author, who polished my roughly worded writings to shine brightly in our readers' hearts and minds.
- My senior leadership team at Bill Hansen Catering, who stood by me, calling me out when I ran off track, and who kept our company profitable during and after COVID. You guys rock!
- Chad Van Allen, my close friend and personal trainer, who has been instrumental in not only my physical health but my mental health, too.
- Guerdy Abraira, star of *Real Housewives of Miami*, who has elevated the art of wedding planning to new heights.
- Jim Allen, chairman of Hard Rock International and CEO of Seminole Gaming, who has trusted my team to provide catering at his home on the New River in Fort Lauderdale.
- Tony Argiz, chairman and CEO of Morrison, Brown, Argiz & Farra, one of the top 40 accounting firms in the country.
- Michael Cheng, dean of the Chaplin School of Hospitality & Tourism Management at Florida International University, who has supported my efforts to fund and create a Catering and Events Lab on the FIU campus.

- Charles Elvan (Chuck) Cobb, CEO of Cobb Partners, former chairman and CEO of Arvida Disney Development Company and former ambassador to Iceland, who has been my role model for decades and a "tell-it-like-it-is" mentor.
- Stuart Gardner, president and CEO of Florida Meeting Services, a loyal client starting in the early 1980s, who has relied on us to delight his clients since then.
- Linda Gassenheimer, a TV and radio personality, journalist, spokesperson, food consultant, and bestselling author of over 12 books, including *The Good Carb Diet for Life* and *Good-Carb Meals in Minutes*.
- Mike Hampton, former dean and professor at the Chaplin School of Hospitality & Tourism Management at Florida International University, who has mentored me over four decades.
- Sherrill Hudson, former managing partner of Deloitte & Touche, member of multiple boards of directors, and current chairman of the Miami Cancer Institute, who has advised me on various business matters as a friend and golfing partner.
- Mike Kady, executive coach and chairman of Peer Group Advisory Boards, who has blessed me with his wisdom, which has resulted in some profitable business decisions.
- David Lawrence, former publisher of the *Miami Herald* and the *Detroit Free Press*, and chairman of the Children's Movement of Florida, who has encouraged me to invest my time, talent, and treasure in Touching Miami with Love, serving children and youth with holistic programming with inspiration, education, and empowerment.
- Allen Morris, author of *All In*, and client since 1980 when I catered his rehearsal dinner at the historic Miami Club. Allen is a leader in many faith-based groups, not only in Miami but worldwide.

- Alex Penelas, former mayor of Miami-Dade County, with whom we share a love for our slice of paradise in South Florida.
- Carl Sacks, executive director of Leading Caterers of America, and managing director of Certified Catering Consultants, who has provided significant financial advice that has contributed to my success.
- David Scheiner, former CEO of Macy's South, who has supported me in several new ventures.
- Peter Schnebly, CEO of Schnebly Redland's Winery, who has supported our efforts in developing relationships in the Homestead/Redland wedding market, South Florida's version of the Napa Valley.
- Allen Susser, CEO of Allen Susser Consulting and Restaurants, who has supported my culinary needs for many decades.

Sara Perez Webber wishes to thank:

- Bill Hansen, for bringing me along on this journey to help craft his inspiring stories. It's been a privilege and a pleasure, Bill!
- Klaas and Antoinette De Waal, publishers of *Catering, Foodservice & Events*, for giving me the opportunity to be the editor of a magazine that's introduced me to some of the most innovative entrepreneurs on the planet.
- Most of all, my family: My parents, June and Mike Perez, who've given me so much love and support; my three sons—Jack, Nick, and Lucas—the lights of my life, who are the inspiration for all that I do; and my husband, Jay, who encourages me, advises me, stands by me, and loves me through all of life's stressful deadlines.

ABOUT THE AUTHORS

Bill Hansen, a 55-year catering veteran, is recognized as a giant in the catering profession. Bill is a Cornell hotel school grad, former U.S. Naval officer, owner of several Miami catering and hospitality companies, and since 1990 an instructor at Florida International University's Chaplin School of Hospitality & Tourism Management, where he is building a catering and events lab on campus for students.

Bill and his team have won numerous awards, including the Lifetime Achievement Award from Catersource and BizBash Caterer of the Year. In 2023, readers of the *Miami Herald* voted Bill Hansen Catering and its exclusive venue Villa Woodbine the "Best of Miami-Dade."

Turning 79 years old in 2025, Bill is not retired but refired. He is a man of faith, courage, conviction, passion, and empathy. His mission with this book is to motivate others to rise to the top of their chosen professions.

Sara Perez Webber is the editor-in-chief of *Catering, Foodservice & Events* (formerly *Catering Magazine*). She has written hundreds of articles about the catering and events industries, interviewing top caterers, chefs, and event planners from across the U.S.

Sara is a graduate of American University in Washington, D.C. For 30 years, she's worked as an editor and writer for magazines, books, and digital media outlets. With a background that includes editorial positions at various travel publications, Sara continues to write freelance travel articles. She lives in South Florida with her husband and three sons.

www.ingramcontent.com/pod-product-compliance
Lightning Source LLC
Chambersburg PA
CBHW030300100526
44590CB00012B/461